SELECT MENU

Browse	⌘-B
Find	⌘-F
Layout	⌘-L
Preview	⌘-U
Find All	⌘-J
Refind	⌘-R
Omit	⌘-M
Omit Multiple	⌘-Shift-M
Define Fields	⌘-Shift-D
Sort	⌘-S

LAYOUT MENU

Align to Grid	⌘-Y
T-Squares	⌘-T

ARRANGE MENU

Group	⌘-G
Ungroup	⌘-Shift-G
Lock	⌘-H
Unlock	⌘-Shift-H
Bring to Front	⌘-Shift-Option-F
Bring Forward	⌘-Shift-F
Send to Back	⌘-Shift-Option-J
Send Backward	⌘-Shift-J
Align Objects	⌘-K
Alignment	⌘-Shift-K

BOOKS THAT WORK JUST LIKE YOUR MAC

As a Macintosh user, you enjoy unique advantages. You enjoy a dynamic user environment. You enjoy the successful integration of graphics, sound, and text. Above all, you enjoy a computer that's fun and easy to use.

When your computer gives you all this, why accept less in your computer books?

At SYBEX, we don't believe you should. That's why we've committed ourselves to publishing the highest quality computer books for Macintosh users. Externally, our books emulate the Mac "look and feel," with powerful, appealing illustrations and easy-to-read pages. Internally, our books stress "why" over "how," so you'll learn concepts, not sequences of steps. Philosophically, our books are designed to help you get work done, not to teach you about computers.

In short, our books are fun and easy to use—just like the Mac. We hope you find them just as enjoyable.

FOR A COMPLETE CATALOG OF OUR PUBLICATIONS:

SYBEX Inc.
2021 Challenger Drive, Alameda, CA 94501
Tel: (510) 523-8233/(800) 227-2346 Telex: 336311
Fax: (510) 523-2373

SYBEX is committed to using natural resources wisely to preserve and improve our environment. As a leader in the computer book publishing industry, we are aware that over 40% of America's solid waste is paper. This is why we have been printing the text of books like this one on recycled paper since 1982.

This year our use of recycled paper will result in the saving of more than 15,300 trees. We will lower air pollution effluents by 54,000 pounds, save 6,300,000 gallons of water, and reduce landfill by 2,700 cubic yards.

In choosing a SYBEX book you are not only making a choice for the best in skills and information, you are also choosing to enhance the quality of life for all of us.

FileMaker Pro 2.0

FOR THE **MAC**

IN A NUTSHELL

FILEMAKER® PRO 2.0
FOR THE MAC®
IN A NUTSHELL

Maria L. Langer

SYBEX®

San Francisco . Paris . Düsseldorf . Soest

Acquisitions Editor: Dianne King
Developmental Editor: Kenyon Brown
Editor: Marilyn Smith
Technical Editor: Mark Taber
Project Editor: Michelle Nance
Book Designer: Helen Bruno
Screen Graphics: John Corrigan, Cuong Le
Page Layout and Typesetting: Len Gilbert
Proofreader/Production Assistant: David Silva
Indexer: Matthew Spence
Cover Designer: Ingalls + Associates
Cover Illustrator: Harumi Kubo

Library of Congress Card Number: 92-83713
ISBN: 0-7821-1214-5

Manufactured in the United States of America
10 9 8 7 6 5 4 3 2 1

To my mother,
my very favorite Macintosh user

ACKNOWLEDGMENTS

Although there might be only one person's name on the cover, it takes more than one person to create a book. I would like to take a moment to acknowledge and thank a few of the folks who had a hand—either directly or indirectly—in this one.

First, the people at SYBEX: Dianne King, Ken Brown, Michelle Nance, Marilyn Smith, and Mark Taber. Dianne got me started, Ken and Michelle got me pointed in the right direction, and Marilyn and Mark made sure my words were just right.

Second, the people at Claris for putting together such a great product. I would especially like to thank Ben in Technical Support for his help when I had nowhere else to turn.

Next, the people who got me started with FileMaker Pro and picked my brain with their questions: Judy Bago, Bette Devito, and Phil Fein. Bette gets additional thanks for planting the seed that led to my relationship with the folks at SYBEX.

Finally, I would like to thank my friends and family for their support: Michael Chilingerian, Tom Heffernan, Ralph Merritt, Madelyn Odendahl, Laura Langer, and Mary Soricelli. Their encouraging words are important to me—more important than they might realize.

Maria L. Langer
Harrington Park, NJ

CONTENTS

AT A GLANCE

CONTENTS

ENTERING AND EDITING DATABASE RECORDS

MODIFYING DATABASE LAYOUTS

MODIFYING LAYOUT PARTS

USING ADVANCED FEATURES

INTRODUCTION

FileMaker Pro is the top-selling database application for the Macintosh. Work with it just ten minutes, and you'll realize why. FileMaker Pro is not only easy to learn and use, but it also offers an incredible amount of flexibility in database design and appearance. Its advanced features, including data summarization, automatic data entry, database lookups, and scripting capabilities, make it an application that grows with you.

WHO SHOULD READ THIS BOOK

This book was designed and written with the new FileMaker Pro user in mind. It starts with the most basic tasks and works its way up to more advanced topics. Each chapter includes introductory material, general information about the topics covered, and illustrated instructions for completing specific tasks.

Even if you've previously worked with FileMaker Pro, you'll find the illustrations and descriptions in this book invaluable. FileMaker Pro version 1.0 users will be introduced to the new features of FileMaker Pro version 2.0. Use the table of contents or index to jump to just the information you need.

WHAT'S NEW IN 2.0

If you haven't upgraded to FileMaker Pro version 2.0 yet, what are you waiting for? Look what you're missing out on:

▸ **Read-only media support:** FileMaker Pro can now open files on locked disks or CD-ROM disks.

▶ **Cross platform file sharing:** With the introduction of a Windows 3.1 version of FileMaker Pro, FileMaker database files can now be shared between Macintosh and Windows computers.

▶ **QuickTime and sound support:** FileMaker Pro's new picture/sound field type lets you paste in QuickTime movies or record sounds (see Chapter 2).

▶ **Access to read-only fields:** FileMaker Pro now allows you to access calculation or summary fields to copy data (see Chapter 3).

▶ **New colors:** FileMaker Pro now offers an additional 7 colors, bringing the total number of colors available up to 88 (see Chapter 4).

▶ **New layouts:** FileMaker Pro now offers two additional layouts: extended columnar reports and templates for Avery labels (see Chapter 6).

▶ **Reserialize a database:** FileMaker Pro now lets you reserialize the contents of any database field (see Chapter 11).

▶ **Field-formatting options:** FileMaker Pro offers two new field-formatting options: scrolling fields and an Other selection (see Chapter 11). In addition, users can now select a field's entire contents when tabbing to that field.

▶ **Improved script and button capabilities:** FileMaker Pro's entire scripting interface has been updated to provide greater control over scripting and buttons (see Chapter 12).

▶ **Export summary information:** FileMaker Pro now allows you to export summary fields (see Chapter 12).

▶ **Preferences:** FileMaker Pro now offers a Preferences dialog box where you can customize general, document, and memory settings (see Chapter 12).

Claris has made additional cosmetic and interface changes to FileMaker Pro; you'll see notes about these minor changes throughout this book.

WHAT'S IN THE BOOK

Here's a summary of the contents of the 12 chapters in this book:

▶ Chapter 1 defines terms like database, record, field, and layout. It also discusses FileMaker Pro's modes and takes a look at the FileMaker Pro document window.

▶ Chapter 2 explains how to create a database from scratch and define fields for it.

▶ Chapter 3 describes how to use Browse mode to enter database information. It also discusses editing records and moving from record to record.

▶ Chapter 4 provides a look at Layout mode. It explains how layout objects work to arrange information on screen and in printed reports and how to change your layouts.

▶ Chapter 5 shows how to work with layout parts to organize information on printed reports.

▶ Chapter 6 describes how to create new layouts from scratch and the uses for each type of layout.

▶ Chapter 7 explores Find mode and explains how to search through a database and select information. You will also learn how to create multiple find requests for more complex searches.

▶ Chapter 8 provides instructions for sorting records by one or more database fields.

▶ Chapter 9 covers previewing and printing reports. You will explore the Page Setup and Print dialog boxes and see the benefits of using Preview mode before printing.

▶ Chapter 10 describes how to use summary fields and parts to summarize data.

▶ Chapter 11 reviews the field-entry options FileMaker Pro offers. These options can automatically enter data, verify entries, and customize data entry.

▶ Chapter 12 describes some of the advanced features of FileMaker Pro, including setting preferences, importing and exporting information, setting access privileges, and creating scripts.

ABOUT THE NOTES

Throughout this book, you'll find different icons marking in-text notes. These notes provide additional information you may find useful. Look for these icons:

 Notes are additional pieces of information to help you work with FileMaker Pro. They explain how FileMaker Pro works.

 Tips are ideas for making the most out of FileMaker Pro.

 For More Information notes point you to places where you can get more information about a topic being covered.

 The New in 2.0 icon points out the features that are new to FileMaker Pro version 2.0.

 Shortcuts are Command key (⌘) alternatives and other techniques that you can use to increase your productivity.

 Warning notes point out important information that could help prevent data loss or costly errors. Keep a sharp eye out for these notes.

FileMaker Pro Database Basics

THIS CHAPTER WILL lay the groundwork for all the chapters that follow. It defines some important database terms and introduces a few of the basics of FileMaker Pro.

If you've never worked with a database before, this chapter is required reading. If you've worked with other databases, read this chapter to learn how FileMaker Pro uses database terminology and applies database concepts. Even if you've worked with FileMaker Pro before, you might want to skim through this chapter to make sure you're familiar with all the terms and concepts.

WHAT IS A DATABASE?

A *database* is a collection of related information. It is usually organized into fields and records. A *field* is a category of information. A *record* is a collection of fields relating to one topic.

An address book is a good example of a database. It usually includes names, addresses, and phone numbers:

Addresses

Name	John Smith		Phone
Address	123 Main Street		201/555-1212
	Cresskill	NJ 07626	
Name	Frank N. Stein		Phone
Address	1313 Mockingbird Lane		201/976-1212
	Bergenfield	NJ 07621	
Name	Johnny B. Goode		Phone
Address	1 Chart Boulevard		213/555-1212
	Hollywood	CA 90547	

You can think of each of these categories of information as a field. All the information for one person or company makes up a record.

With FileMaker Pro, you create database fields and then enter information into them for each record. You can have any number of fields or records in your database, and add or delete them at any time. You can also sort, search, display, and print your records in a wide variety of ways, as you will learn in this book.

WHAT IS A LAYOUT?

FileMaker Pro displays and prints database information based on layouts. A *layout* is an arrangement of fields and other design elements (such as field labels and graphics) that governs the way information is presented on screen or paper.

A database can have any number of layouts, each with any number or combination of fields. Think of a layout as a report format. The contents of the fields for each record don't differ from layout to layout, but the fields displayed and their arrangement may.

Here's the same address book database you saw in the previous section, but displayed in two different layouts:

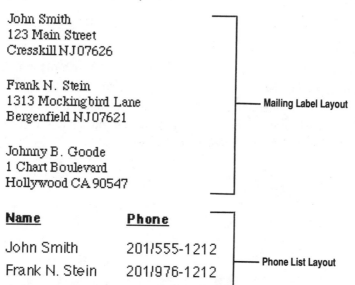

John Smith
123 Main Street
Cresskill NJ 07626

Frank N. Stein
1313 Mockingbird Lane
Bergenfield NJ 07621

Johnny B. Goode
1 Chart Boulevard
Hollywood CA 90547

—— Mailing Label Layout

<u>Name</u>	<u>Phone</u>	
John Smith	201/555-1212	
Frank N. Stein	201/976-1212	—— Phone List Layout
Johnny B. Goode	213/555-1212	

As you can see, the fields included and their arrangement depend on the purpose of the layout.

Each FileMaker Pro database file includes not only the information contained in its database fields, but the instructions the program needs to display that information in the layouts you create.

WORKING IN FILEMAKER PRO MODES

FileMaker Pro has four *modes*: Browse, Find, Layout, and Preview. Each mode lets you work with different features of the program. You can switch from mode to mode with commands on the Select menu.

 NEW IN 2.0
An indicator at the bottom of the FileMaker Pro window shows the current mode. This indicator is also a pop-up menu that lets you access all four modes.

BROWSE MODE

Browse is the mode you use to view, create, edit, and delete records. You can view records one at a time or as a list, depending on the layout. Each field is an edit box in which you can enter and change information. Commands on the Edit menu let you create, duplicate, and delete records. Although you can view records in Preview mode, you can change them only in Browse mode.

Browse mode looks like this:

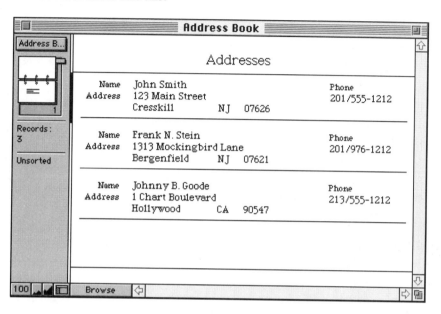

Notice the mode indicator at the bottom of the window, which lets you know that FileMaker Pro is in Browse mode.

FIND MODE

Find is the mode you use to define the information you want to find in a database and perform the search. Each field is an edit box in which you can enter criteria for the search. Commands on the Edit menu let you create or duplicate search criteria.

Find mode looks like this:

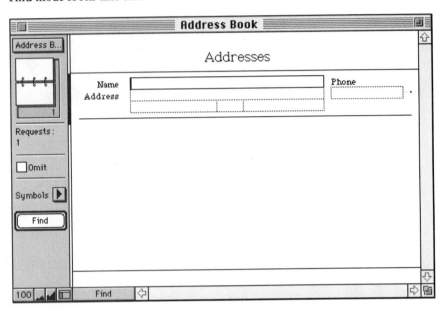

After you have specified the criteria, you can click on the Find button to perform the search. FileMaker Pro displays the records it found and returns to Browse mode so you can work with the results.

LAYOUT MODE

Layout is the mode you use to view, create, and modify database layouts. You can move or modify each object, such as fields and field labels, within the FileMaker Pro window. Use the mouse to reposition, stretch, squeeze, or select objects. Use commands on the Format menu to change the font, font size, style, or color of objects. Commands on the Edit menu let you create, duplicate, or delete the current layout.

Layout mode looks like this:

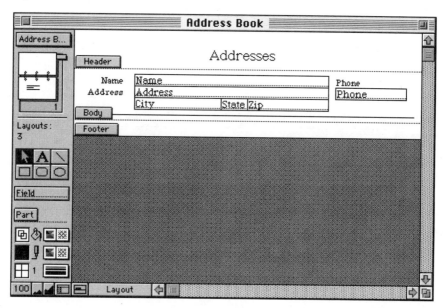

When you have finished making adjustments to a layout, you can check your changes in Browse or Preview mode.

PREVIEW MODE

Preview is the mode you use to view documents before printing them. Preview mode shows exactly how your document will appear when printed. Although Browse mode lets you see the records of a database, it does not show each separate page of a printed report. In addition, some layout features, such as headers and footers, are not accurately represented in Browse mode.

Preview mode looks like this:

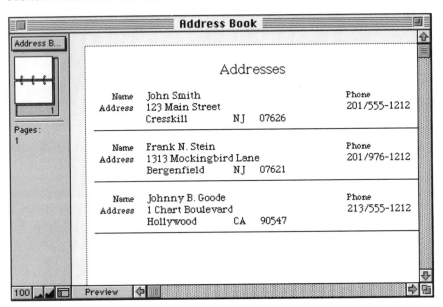

You can save a lot of paper by using Preview mode rather than printing test copies of your documents.

THE FILEMAKER PRO DOCUMENT WINDOW

FileMaker Pro's document window contains a mixture of familiar Macintosh elements and FileMaker Pro tools and controls. The Macintosh elements—title bar, scroll bars, scroll arrows, scroll boxes, close box, zoom box, and size box—remain the same from window to window and work just as they do in any other Macintosh application. However, the appearance and function of some of FileMaker Pro's tools and controls change depending on the current FileMaker Pro mode.

FOR MORE INFORMATION...
If you're not familiar with the standard window elements discussed here, consult the reference manuals that came with your Macintosh.

THE STATUS AREA

The FileMaker Pro window status area appears on its left side:

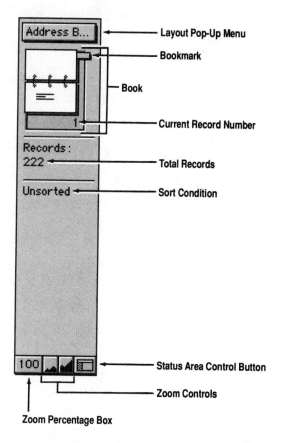

Let's take a moment to look at some of the status area's tools and controls:

‣ **Layout pop-up menu:** The Layout pop-up menu is at the top of the status area. It always shows the name of the current layout. When you click on it, a menu of other existing layouts pops up.

‣ **Book:** The book is beneath the Layout pop-up menu. It lets you scroll through records, find requests, layouts, or pages, depending on the current mode (Browse, Find, Layout, or Preview, respectively).

‣ **Zoom control buttons:** At the bottom of every FileMaker Pro window are the zoom controls. The two icons that look like mountains make the screen image smaller or larger. The zoom percentage button shows the percent of magnification. Images can be as small as 25 percent or as large as 400 percent of normal document size. These buttons work in every mode.

‣ **Status area control button:** To the right of the zoom controls is the status area control button. This button hides or displays the status area.

You'll learn how to use these tools in the following chapters.

LAYOUT TOOLS AND CONTROLS

In Layout mode, the status area fills with a number of layout tools and controls:

These buttons let you customize your layouts. Layout tools are discussed in greater detail in Chapter 4.

IN THIS CHAPTER, you learned the meanings of several important database terms, such as database, field, and record. We discussed layouts and how File-Maker Pro uses them to display or print database contents. We also looked at File-Maker Pro's four modes and some of the components of its document windows. The basic concepts we covered will be used throughout this book.

In the next chapter, we'll launch FileMaker Pro, create a new database from scratch, and define fields to hold information.

2

Creating a Database and Defining Fields

FEATURING

- Planning a database
- Creating a new database file
- Defining fields
- Creating a calculation field
- Changing field definitions

CREATING A
DATABASE AND DEFINING FIELDS
....

CH. 2

AS YOU LEARNED in the previous chapter, fields are one of the basic building blocks of a database file. They're like paint buckets, but instead of holding different colors of paint, they hold different categories of information.

You can create a new file as soon as you open FileMaker Pro or after you've been working in the program. But before you start setting up the database file, you should take the time to plan your database design.

DESIGNING A DATABASE

Although FileMaker Pro is flexible enough to let you create database files "on the fly," it's a good idea to plan your database before you create it. This could save you the time and effort of changing the database later on. It isn't necessary to spend a lot of time making elaborate plans, but you should know, at a minimum, the fields you want to include in the database.

Before even launching FileMaker Pro, take a moment to write down all the fields you expect to need. There might be more of them than you realize.

For example, if you're creating an address book database, you'll need fields for each person's name and address. But do you want to keep the name in one field or split it into two? If you plan to sort the records by last name, you'll probably want two name fields, one for the first name and one for the last. And how about the address? Although you can include as many lines as you like in a text field, if you plan to sort information by city or zip code, you'll need to put them in separate fields. These are the kinds of things you should consider when planning the fields to include in your database.

CREATING A NEW DATABASE FILE

After you know what fields you want to include in your database, you're ready to create the database file. In FileMaker Pro, you can create a new file when you first open FileMaker Pro, or by using the New command on the File menu.

CREATING A NEW FILE WHEN
YOU FIRST LAUNCH FILEMAKER PRO

When you first launch FileMaker Pro, it gives you an opportunity to create a new file. Unlike many other applications, FileMaker Pro prompts you for a file name when you *create* a file rather than when you first *save* it. This is because File-Maker Pro saves the file automatically as you work. If you don't give the file a name right from the start, FileMaker Pro won't be able to save it.

FOR MORE INFORMATION...
If you're not sure how to launch (or open) a Macintosh application, consult the reference manuals that came with your Macintosh.

Launch FileMaker Pro by double-clicking on its application icon. FileMaker Pro's splash screen appears briefly. It shows the program name, your registration information, and various trademark and copyright notices. Then you'll see an Open File dialog box similar to this one:

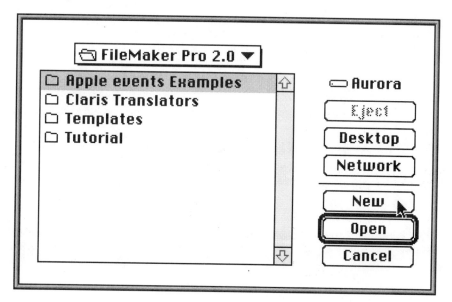

Click on the New button. This tells FileMaker Pro that you want to create a new
database file. A standard Save As dialog box appears:

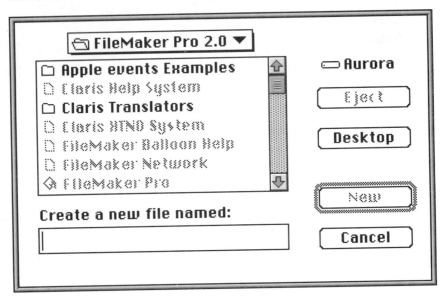

Enter a file name in the edit box beneath the prompt

Create a new file named:

Then click on the New button.

FileMaker Pro creates a new file with the name you provided. It then displays the
dialog box for defining your database fields, which we'll discuss in a moment.

CREATING A FILE WHEN FILEMAKER PRO IS OPEN

If FileMaker Pro is already open, select the New command from the File menu to
create a new database file. A standard Save As dialog box appears. Enter a name
for the new file and click on New.

FileMaker Pro creates a new file with the name you provided and displays the
Define Fields dialog box.

DEFINING FIELDS

Before you can enter information into a database, you must define fields to hold that information. Whenever you choose to create a new database, FileMaker Pro displays the Define Fields dialog box. In this dialog box, you name each field and specify its type.

NOTE

You can access the Define Fields dialog box at any time by selecting Define Fields from the Select menu.

FileMaker Pro provides seven different types of fields. You can store each type of information—text, numbers, dates, graphics, and so on—in an appropriate field type. Then you can format a field for the specific type of information it contains. Formatting fields will be discussed in Chapter 4.

You can choose from these types of fields:

- A text field can contain any characters you can type. You can enter up to 64,000 characters in this type of field.

- A number field can also contain any characters you can type, but the amount of information you can enter is limited to one line of up to 255 characters. Number fields usually contain numerical data that will be used in calculations.

- A date field can contain a date.

- A time field can contain a time.

- A picture or sound field can contain graphics or sounds. You can paste graphics from the clipboard or from an imported graphic file into a field. Sounds can be recorded right in FileMaker Pro or imported from a sound file into a field.

NEW IN 2.0

Sound support has been added to the picture field type. To record sounds in FileMaker Pro, however, your Macintosh must have sound-recording capabilities.

▶ A calculation field will contain the result of a calculation. When you create a calculation field, you are prompted for a formula. We will discuss calculation fields later in this chapter.

▶ A summary field will contain the result of a formula calculated for a group of records. This makes it possible to summarize information in a database. Summary fields will be covered in Chapter 10.

THE DEFINE FIELDS DIALOG BOX

The Define Fields dialog box looks like this:

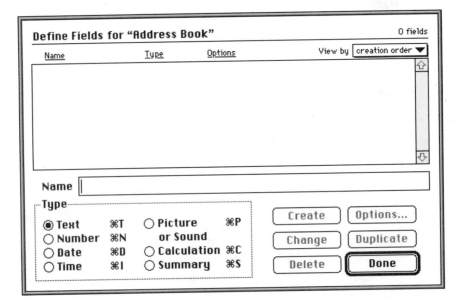

NEW IN 2.0

The total number of defined fields now appears in the upper-right corner of the Define Fields dialog box. The View By menu now appears beside the words View By rather than under an icon representing two index cards, but it offers the same options.

Let's take a look at the parts of this dialog box:

- **Field list window**: The field list, a scrollable window, takes up most of the space in the Define Fields dialog box. The window displays the name, type, and options (if any) for each field. Field options will be covered in Chapter 11.

- **View By menu:** Above the field list is the View By pop-up menu. It lets you change the order of the fields. Click on the menu to see the four options: creation order, field name, field type, and custom order.

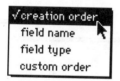

- **Name edit box:** Beside the word *Name* is a long edit box in which you enter the name for each new field.

- **Type buttons:** Below the Name box are the Type radio buttons for each of the seven field types listed above.

- **Action buttons:** The action buttons in this dialog box let you create, change, delete, specify options, or define access privileges for fields. If the button is gray, it cannot be used.

- **Done button:** The Done button tells FileMaker Pro to accept all your changes and remove the dialog box.

CREATING A FIELD

In the Name box, enter the name of the field you want to create. Field names can be up to 60 characters long. If you plan to use a field in a calculation, its name may not include any of these symbols or reserved words: +, -, *, /, ^, &, =, ≠, >, <, ≥, ≤, (,), AND, OR, NOT, TODAY, or the name of a FileMaker Pro function.

Click on the button beside the type of field you want to create, and then click on the Create button. The field you defined appears in the field list window, and its name appears highlighted in the Name box.

SHORTCUT
Beside each field type is a Command-key alternative you can use to select that field type. For example, if you want to create a date field, hold down the ⌘ key and press D.

To enter the next field's name, type over the name in the Name box. Then choose a field type and click on Create. Use the same procedure to define the rest of the fields in your database. Each field you create appears in the field list window. When you're finished, the Define Fields dialog box may look something like this:

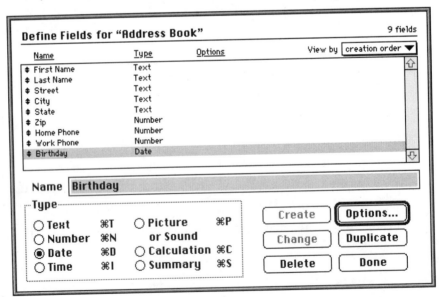

You can rearrange the order of the fields in the field list. To move a field up or down in the list, drag the double-arrow icon to the left of that field.

SETTING UP CALCULATION FIELDS

A calculation field lets you calculate a value for each record based on data in that record and formulas you create. Use this type of field to perform mathematical operations on values in other fields. For example, create a Total field to add up the contents of some other fields. Create an Extended Price field to multiply a Unit Price field by a Number of Units field. Create a Sales Tax field to multiply the state sales tax rate by a Subtotal field.

Calculation fields eliminate the need to manually perform calculations in your databases. Just set up the calculation once and let FileMaker Pro do the work.

THE CALCULATION DIALOG BOX

After you've named the field, clicked on the Calculation radio button, and clicked on Create, the Calculation dialog box appears:

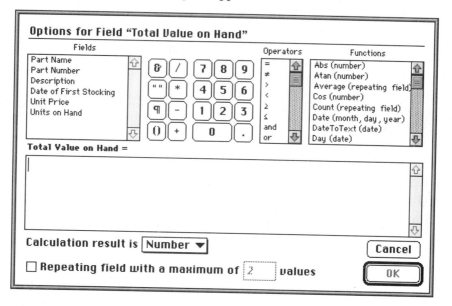

This dialog box has several major parts:

♦ **Formula box:** In the Formula box, you write and edit your formula. When you first create a calculation field, the Formula box is empty. You can write formulas by selecting options in the dialog box or by typing part or all of the formula in the Formula box.

- **Fields list:** The Fields list includes all the fields in the database. Double-click on a field name to include it in a calculation.

- **Mathematical symbol buttons:** Four of the eight buttons in this group cover standard mathematical operations: addition (+), subtraction (−), multiplication (*), and division (/). The parentheses button lets you indicate the order of formula operations. The other three buttons are text operators that work with text in formulas. Click once on a button to include it in a calculation.

- **Number buttons:** The number buttons are laid out like a numeric keypad. They let you include numbers in formulas. Click once on a button to include the number in a calculation.

- **Operators list:** The list of operators includes a number of operators for comparisons (=, ≠, >, <, ≥, and ≤), logic (AND, OR, and NOT), and arithmetic (^). All of these operators can be used in formulas. Double-click on an operator to include it in a calculation.

- **Functions list:** The list of functions includes 61 functions, which perform a wide variety of mathematical and text calculations. Many of FileMaker Pro's functions will be familiar to you if you have worked with spreadsheets.

NEW IN 2.0
Along with each function, the Functions list now includes a note about how to use that function in a field.

- **Calculation Result pop-up menu:** The results of a calculation can be text, a number, a date, or a time. The Calculation Result pop-up menu lets you tell FileMaker Pro which type of result to provide. In most cases, a calculation will result in a number.

- **Repeating field boxes:** Repeating fields make it possible to have more than one value in a field. To make a calculation field into a repeating field, click on this check box and indicate the number of values you want to be able to place in that field. Repeating fields will be discussed in Chapter 11.

DEFINING A CALCULATION

To define a calculation, click on field names, mathematical symbols, numbers, operators, and functions as needed to write a formula. You can use standard Macintosh editing techniques to make changes to the formula you create.

Functions are preset calculations. They can be broken down into separate parts: the function name and one or more *parameters* (sometimes known as *arguments*) enclosed in parentheses and separated with commas. The function name tells FileMaker Pro what to do. The parameters tell it what to work with. The commas keep the parameters separated, and the parentheses identify where a function's list of parameters begin and end.

When you're finished writing your formula, it might look something like this:

Total Value on Hand =

```
Unit Price * Units on Hand
```

If necessary, use the Calculation Result pop-up menu to change the type of result. If this is to be a repeating field, click on the Repeating Field check box and enter the number of values in the Repeating Fields edit box.

When you click on OK to accept the formula, you are returned to the Define Fields dialog box. The formula you created for the field appears in the Options column in the field list window:

CREATING A
DATABASE AND DEFINING FIELDS
. . . .

CH. 2

Here are some other examples of formulas you can create with FileMaker Pro, including some that use functions:

PURPOSE OF FIELD	FIELD NAMES IN CALCULATION	FILEMAKER PRO FORMULA
Multiply an invoice subtotal by the sales tax	Subtotal, Sales Tax Rate	Subtotal * Sales Tax Rate
Add the total sales tax to an invoice subtotal	Subtotal, Sales Tax Amount	Subtotal + Sales Tax Amount
Calculate the average of a salesperson's monthly sales amounts	January Sales, February Sales, March Sales	(January Sales + February Sales + March Sales)/3
Find the name of the day of the week of a date (a text result)	Date	DayName (Date)
Calculate the annual payment for a loan	Principal, Interest Rate, Term	PMT (Principal, Interest Rate, Term)
Calculate the monthly payment for a loan	Principal, Interest Rate, Term	PMT (Principal, Interest Rate / 12, Term * 12)
Calculate the monthly payment for a loan rounded to dollars and cents	Principal, Interest Rate, Term	Round (PMT (Principal, Interest Rate / 12, Term * 12), 2)
Write a sentence that says to pay an amount by a date (a text result)	Monthly Payment, Date	"Please Pay $" & Monthly Payment & " by " & DateToText(Date) & "."

MODIFYING A FIELD DEFINITION

Once a field has been created, its definition is not set in stone. You can change the field name, type, or options at any time.

To modify a field definition, click on the name of the field in the Define Fields dialog box. Then make changes as follows:

- To change the field name, edit the contents of the Name box.

- To change the field type, click on a different Type radio button.

- To change the options for a field, click on the Options button, edit the options as necessary, and click on OK to accept your changes.

When you're finished editing the field definition, click on the Change button. Depending on the type of change you made, you may see a warning dialog box explaining the consequences of the change. For example, you'll see this warning if you try to change a number field to a calculation field:

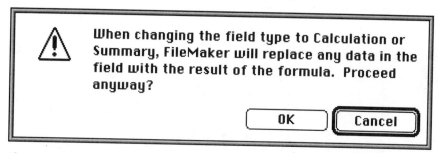

If you try to change a text field to a number field, you'll see this warning:

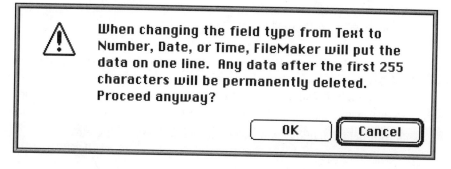

You can confirm or cancel your change in any warning dialog box that appears.

After you click on Change and confirm your changes if necessary, the new field definition appears in the field list window.

DELETING A FIELD

You can delete a field from your database at any time. Deleting a field from a database is very different from deleting a field from a layout. See Chapter 4 for information about removing fields from layouts.

To delete a field, click on the name of that field in the Define Fields dialog box, and then click on the Delete button. You'll see this warning:

WARNING
Deleting a field from a database deletes all the data stored in that field for every record. You cannot use the Undo command on the Edit menu to restore the field. Be sure that you really do want to delete a field before you click on the Delete button.

If you're sure you want to delete the field, click on the Delete button, and the field will be removed from the field list.

ACCEPTING YOUR FIELD DEFINITIONS

When you're finished defining fields and are ready to enter data into your database, click on the Done button in the Define Fields dialog box. This accepts all your field definitions and closes the Define Fields dialog box.

IN THIS CHAPTER, we created a new database file and defined fields to hold information. Along the way, we learned about the seven kinds of fields FileMaker Pro supports. We took a close look at the Define Fields and Calculation dialog boxes. We also learned how to modify and delete fields. You can use the techniques covered in this chapter to create and modify fields in your database.

In the next chapter, we'll start to fill the database with information. We'll see how to enter and edit database information, how to create and delete records, and how to move from record to record. These are some of the skills you'll use most when working with FileMaker Pro.

ENTERING AND EDITING DATABASE RECORDS

CREATING A DATABASE file and defining fields for it are just preliminary steps for building a database file. What good is a database if it doesn't contain any information? FileMaker Pro lets you create enormous databases, taking up to 32 megabytes of disk space (or the amount of disk storage space you have available). In this chapter, you'll learn how to fill a database with information, field by field and record by record.

Before we get started, however, let's take a look at the standard layout that appears when you finish defining fields. This is the layout you'll probably use to enter database information.

THE STANDARD LAYOUT

After you've defined all the fields you need, you're ready to enter data into your new database. Clicking on the Done button in the Define Fields dialog box dismisses the box and puts you in Browse mode in your database file. You'll see that FileMaker Pro has automatically created a layout that includes all the fields you created. This is the *standard layout*, and FileMaker Pro calls it *Layout #1*. It might look something like this:

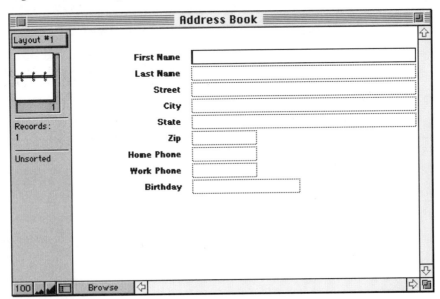

The standard layout has two main components: *field labels* and *field boxes* (or just plain *fields*). Field labels display field names, which identify the fields beside them. The field boxes are where you actually enter information into your database. They are sized according to the field's type. For example, text fields are larger than number or date fields. You can customize any part of the standard layout. Chapter 4 describes how to modify layouts.

When you first create a database, FileMaker Pro not only provides a layout you can use to enter data, but it also creates a blank record. You can tell how many records are in your database and what the current record number is by consulting the book and the area immediately below it:

The number of records changes as your database grows.

ENTERING INFORMATION

You must be in Browse mode to enter or edit database information. Check the mode indicator at the bottom of the screen to make sure it says Browse. If it doesn't, use its pop-up menu to select Browse, or choose Browse from the Select menu.

SHORTCUT
You can switch to Browse mode from any mode by pressing the
⌘–B key combination.

FILLING IN THE FIRST RECORD

If the field boxes do not appear beside the field names in Browse mode, press the Tab key once. The boxes appear, and a blinking insertion point appears in the first field box. The field containing the blinking insertion point is called the *current field*. This field has a solid-line boundary; the other fields have dotted-line boundaries. You can always click in a field to make it the current field.

NEW IN 2.0
With version 2.0, you can access a calculation or another "read-only" field by clicking on the contents of the field. This makes it possible to copy the results of a formula for a calculation field to the clipboard and use it elsewhere. The contents of these fields, however, still cannot be modified.

If you have any calculation or summary fields in your database, field boxes will not appear beside their field labels:

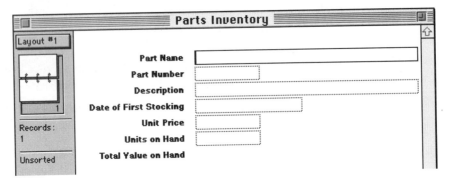

Since FileMaker Pro fills in these fields automatically (according to the formulas you defined when you created them), you don't enter data directly into them.

Type in the data for the first field. A field box is nothing more than a Macintosh edit box. You can enter any data from your keyboard, use the Delete key to back up over mistakes, and even highlight text to be deleted or typed over.

You can also use FileMaker Pro's data-entry shortcuts for common information. These include ⌘-- for the current date, ⌘-; for the current time, and ⌘-' for the contents of the same field in the previous record.

If a field box is too small to hold everything you enter into it, the box temporarily expands to display all the information in it, like this:

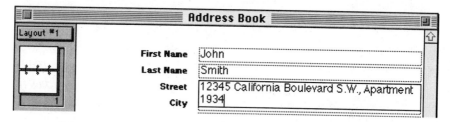

When you move to another field, the field box collapses to its original size. If it is a text field, its contents will appear to be *truncated*, or cut off. If it is a number, calculation, or summary field, a question mark may appear in the field box. Your entire entry is stored, but it will not fit on the layout as it is currently set up.

When a field box is not large enough for the information it must contain, you should enlarge the field so that you can see all of its contents. You can change the size of fields in Layout mode, as explained in Chapter 4.

After you enter data in the first field, press the Tab key to make the next field the current field (but pressing Tab won't make a calculation field the current field).

Continue to fill in each field in this manner. When you press the Tab key after filling in the last field, the first field becomes the current field again.

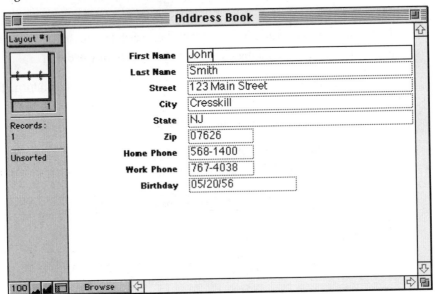

EDITING INFORMATION

You can go back and edit the contents of a field at any time. Use the mouse pointer to drag through a field or portion of a field that needs to be changed. Whatever you drag through is highlighted:

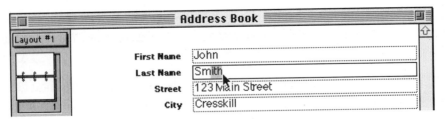

In a field box, you can use all the standard Macintosh editing techniques and commands, including Copy and Paste. Use the Delete key to delete highlighted information, and then type new information to replace it. Or simply type new information over highlighted information.

When you press the Tab key, click elsewhere in the database layout, or move to another record or mode, FileMaker Pro accepts the changes.

NOTE

Until FileMaker Pro accepts the changes you make to a field, calculation fields that depend on that field will not change.

CREATING A NEW RECORD

Since most people aren't interested in creating and maintaining one-record databases, it's a good idea to know how to create new records.

To create a new record, select New from the Edit menu. A blank record appears. Note the changes to the book on the left side of FileMaker Pro's window.

SHORTCUT

In Browse mode, press the ⌘-N key combination to create a new record.

Enter and edit information in the new record as described in the previous sections.

DUPLICATING AN EXISTING RECORD

Sometimes, two records will share a lot of the same information. For example, two people may live at the same address and have the same home phone number, but you want to enter them both into your database as separate records. FileMaker Pro lets you copy existing records to save data-entry time.

To copy the current record, select Duplicate Record from the Edit menu. At first, you might not notice a difference; it seems as if the same record is showing. But if you look at the book in the status area, you will see that another record has been added to the database and that it is the current record.

SHORTCUT
In Browse mode, press the ⌘–D key combination to duplicate the current record.

You can edit the new record as necessary to reflect the correct information.

MOVING FROM RECORD TO RECORD

When you have more than one record, you'll notice another change to the book: one or both of its pages has lines on it. If the top page has lines, this means that there are records before the current record. If the bottom page of the book has lines on it, there are records after the current record. If both pages have lines on them, there are records before *and* after the current record.

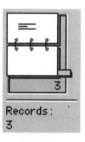

Records Before
Current Record

Records After
Current Record

Records Before and
After Current Record

You can use the book to move from record to record in three ways:

‣ **Clicking on the book pages**: To go to the next record, click on the bottom page of the book. This will only work if the bottom page has lines on it. To go to the previous record, click on the top page of the book. This will only work if the top page has lines on it. The record number changes each time you click.

▸ **Sliding the bookmark:** The horizontal bar on the right side of the book is called the *bookmark*. Slide the bookmark up or down with your mouse pointer to move quickly from one record to another. Release the bookmark when the record number displayed at the bottom of the book is the one you want. (Of course, you need to know the record number you want for this method to be useful.)

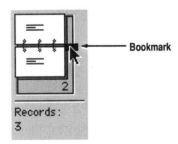

Bookmark

TIP
Remember, you can always see the current record number in the lower-right corner of the book.

▸ **Changing the current record number:** You can also go to another record by changing the current record number that appears at the bottom of the book. Click on that number and type in a new number. Press Return, and the record number you specified appears in the window. (Again, you need to know the record number you want for this method to be useful.)

SHORTCUT
In Browse mode, the ⌘–Tab and ⌘–Shift-Tab key combinations move forward and backward, respectively, through the records.

DELETING A RECORD

SHORTCUT
In Browse mode, press the ⌘–E key combination to delete a record.

If you no longer need an existing record, you can delete it at any time. To delete a record, move to that record, and then select Delete from the Edit menu. You will see this warning dialog box:

If you're sure you want to delete the record, click on the Delete button. Deleting a record *cannot* be undone, so be sure you really do want to delete the record before you click on Delete. FileMaker Pro removes the record and all the data it contains from the database.

CLOSING AND OPENING FILES

As you work with FileMaker Pro, you'll need to know how to close and open existing files. If you've worked with a Macintosh before, you're probably familiar with the methods for handling files, since these are standard Macintosh procedures.

NOTE
The Apple Human Interface Guidelines are a set of rules created by Apple Computer, Inc. They describe how Macintosh applications should work. It is because of these rules that there are standard methods for closing files, opening files, and quitting an application, as well as performing other tasks.

CLOSING A FILE

WARNING
Do not shut off your Macintosh before closing any open FileMaker Pro documents. Doing so may result in damaged files.

You can close a database file in one of two ways:

▸ Select Close from the File menu. This closes the topmost window.

▸ Click on the window's Close box (the small box at the far left side of the title bar).

SHORTCUT

In any mode, the ⌘-W key combination closes the active document window.

Unlike other applications, FileMaker Pro will never ask whether it should save changes to a file before closing it. Remember, FileMaker Pro automatically saves a file as you work with it.

OPENING AN EXISTING FILE

You can also open an existing FileMaker Pro file in one of two ways:

▶ From the Finder, double-click on a FileMaker Pro document icon to launch FileMaker Pro and open that file.

▶ From FileMaker Pro, select Open from the File menu to see a standard Open File dialog box. Select the file you want to open and click on Open. (For more information about using the standard Macintosh Open File dialog box, consult the reference manuals that came with your Macintosh.)

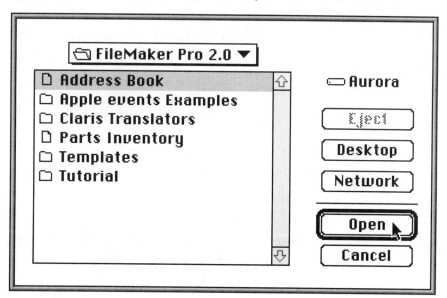

SHORTCUT

In any mode, the ⌘–O key combination lets you open a database file.

QUITTING FILEMAKER PRO

To quit FileMaker Pro, simply select Quit from the File menu. FileMaker Pro closes all open documents and quits.

SHORTCUT

In any mode, press the ⌘–Q key combination to leave FileMaker Pro.

Always use the Shut Down command under the Finder's Special menu to shut down your Macintosh. This makes sure that any open documents and applications are properly closed before your Macintosh is turned off. (For more information about shutting off your Macintosh, consult the manuals that came with it.)

IN THIS CHAPTER, you learned how to store information in a database file. We covered filling in the fields of a record, editing fields, creating new records, duplicating records, moving among records, and deleting records. We also reviewed how to close files, open existing files, and quit FileMaker Pro. With the information in this chapter, you can easily fill a database file with your information.

In the next chapter, you'll learn how to change the layout of a database. As you'll see, FileMaker Pro makes it simple to customize the appearance of a database so it looks just the way you want it to on the screen or in printed reports.

MODIFYING DATABASE LAYOUTS

IN THIS CHAPTER, we'll cover how to customize the appearance of database files. So far, we've spent most of our time in Browse mode, which lets you enter and edit database contents. Now we'll switch to Layout mode, which we glimpsed briefly in Chapter 1.

In Layout mode, FileMaker Pro allows you to modify any layout element, or *object*. You can change an object's position, size, shape, color, font, or format. You can also use FileMaker Pro's layout tools to add objects, such as text, graphics, and fields. You'll find that the flexibility of layouts is one of the most powerful features of FileMaker Pro.

DESIGNING A LAYOUT

Just as you should take a few moments to consider the fields you want to include in a new database file, you should also plan a new layout before you begin to make changes. Again, it isn't necessary to make elaborate plans, but you should know which fields you want to include and where you want them to appear on the layout. Remember, everything that appears on a layout can be modified. Consider the following questions:

- Do you want to move or resize fields?

- Where do you want the fields to go?

- How big do you want the fields to be?

- Do you want to reposition or edit field labels? If so, how?

- Do you want to add lines, graphics, or additional text?

Sketch the layout design you have in mind on a piece of scrap paper. Be sure to draw in the elements you want to add so you remember to include them. Not only does this give you a "plan of attack," but it also lets you see what your layout will look like before you start making changes.

SWITCHING TO LAYOUT MODE

After you know what you want to do, you're ready to modify the layout. To make any changes to a layout, you must be in Layout mode.

You can switch to Layout mode in one of two ways:

▸ Select Layout from the Select menu.

▸ Select Layout from the Mode pop-up menu (at the bottom of the FileMaker Pro window).

SHORTCUT

In any mode, the ⌘-L key combination switches to Layout mode.

When you switch to Layout mode, the status area along the left side of the window changes. If the status area doesn't appear when you are in Layout mode, click on the status area control button at the bottom of the document window.

The status area is filled with a number of layout tools for changing layout elements and adding text, graphics, fields, and parts.

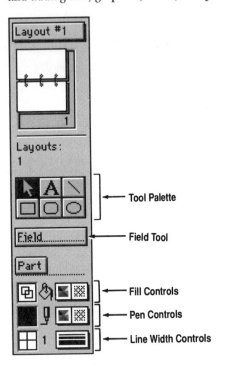

What you might not immediately notice when you first switch to Layout mode is how the book changes. Instead of indicating the number of records as it does in Browse mode, the book shows the number of layouts. If you have more than one layout, you can move from layout to layout by using the Layout pop-up menu above the book or the book itself. (Moving from layout to layout is covered in Chapter 6.)

WORKING WITH LAYOUT OBJECTS

In the document window, you see the layout objects rather than the contents of the database. An *object* is a layout element, such as a field, text (including field labels), or graphics. In Layout mode, a field normally appears as a field box containing the field name (or as much of it as will fit in the box) on a dotted *baseline*. The baseline is useful for helping you align fields and field labels. Text and graphics normally appear without any special boxes around them. In Layout mode, you'll also see *part labels* and *part boundaries*. We'll work with layout *parts* in Chapter 5.

TIP

In Layout mode, it's difficult to tell what your layout will look like when it's printed. To see the layout as it will print, switch to Preview mode. (See Chapter 9 for more about Preview mode.)

SELECTING LAYOUT OBJECTS

In order to change a layout object, you must select it first. To select, resize, or move an object, you use the pointer tool, which is the default tool on the tool palette.

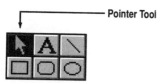

Pointer Tool

If the pointer tool isn't selected, click once on it to select it.

An object is selected when little boxes, called *handles*, appear at its corners to mark its boundaries.

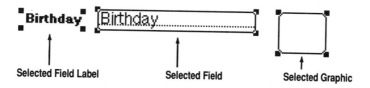

Selected Field Label   Selected Field   Selected Graphic

To deselect any selected layout object, click outside that object's boundaries.

SELECTING A SINGLE OBJECT

The most basic way to select an object is to click on it. Position the pointer over the object, and then click once to select it. You will see handles around it, indicating that it is selected.

You can also select an object by dragging the pointer around it. Position the pointer above and to the left of the object, press the mouse button down, and drag the mouse diagonally across the object. A dotted line selection box appears around the object.

When the selection box *completely surrounds* the object, release the mouse button. Handles appear to show that it has been selected.

SELECTING MULTIPLE OBJECTS

You can use the selection box method to select more than one object. Just drag a selection box around all the objects you want to select.

WARNING
When you're using the Shift-click method to select objects, be sure you release the mouse button after clicking on each object. If you drag the mouse to the second object rather than just click on it, you may move the first object.

Another way to select several objects is by *Shift-clicking* on them. Click on the first object to select it and display its handles. Then, while holding down the Shift key, click on the second object to select it and display its handles as well. Continue to Shift-click on each object you want to include until all of them are selected.

To select *all* the objects on a layout, use the Select All command on the Edit menu. Then you can deselect certain objects by holding down the Shift key and clicking on each of them.

SHORTCUT

In Layout mode, press the ⌘–A key combination to select all the objects in a layout.

RESIZING AND RESHAPING LAYOUT OBJECTS

If a field is not large enough to hold all the information it contains, that information will appear truncated in Browse mode when the field is not the current one. When a field is bigger than it needs to be, it takes up valuable space on your layout. In Layout mode, you can easily resize fields and other objects to suit your needs.

To resize a field or another object, first select it by using one of the techniques described in the previous sections. Then position the pointer over a handle (the lower-right handle is usually the best choice for resizing fields) and press the mouse button. To enlarge the object, drag to the right. To shrink the object, drag to the left.

When the object appears to be the right size, release the mouse button. The object will expand or contract to that size.

Along with changing the horizontal dimensions of a field, you can also resize a field vertically. When you make a text field taller, you can include multiple lines of information within it.

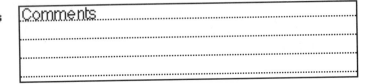

MOVING LAYOUT OBJECTS

When you modify a layout, you will probably want to reposition objects. Moving objects allows you to change the order and organization of fields, field labels, other text, and graphics.

WARNING

Do not place the mouse pointer on top of one of the object's selection handles. If you do, you may resize the object when you try to move it.

To move an object, position the pointer *on* the object to be moved. Press the mouse button down and drag the object to move it. As you move a field or text, its baseline and outline remain visible to help you align it with other objects.

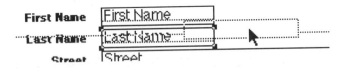

When the object is in the desired position, release the mouse button. The object will appear in its new position.

To move an object a tiny bit at a time, select the object and use the arrow keys on the keyboard to move it one *pixel* at a time. (Pixels, or *picture elements*, are the dots that make up the screen image.)

REMOVING OBJECTS FROM A LAYOUT

Occasionally, you may want to remove one or more objects from a layout. You might not need a particular field label, or you may not want to include all the fields.

NOTE

Removing or adding fields in a layout is very different from removing or adding fields in the database. Chapter 2 describes how to delete or insert fields in a database file.

To delete an object, select the object or group of objects you want to remove and press the Delete key. The selected objects will be removed from the current layout, but not from the database file itself.

ADDING FIELDS TO A LAYOUT

To add existing fields to your layout, you use the field tool, which is beneath the tool palette in the status area. Position your mouse pointer over the field tool, press the mouse button down, and drag the tool onto the layout. The field tool itself does not move, but a field outline, complete with baseline, appears on the layout.

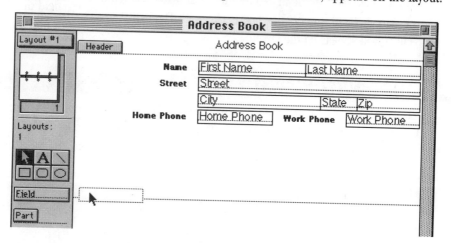

MODIFYING
DATABASE LAYOUTS
. . . .

CH. 4

When the field outline is in the desired position on your layout, release the mouse button. You will see the New Field dialog box.

This dialog box contains a window that lists all the existing fields in your database.

In the New Field window, click once on the field you want to add to select it. If you want a field name to be added to the layout just to the left of the field, make sure the Create Field Label check box is checked. Then click on OK. The field you chose will appear on the layout.

WORKING WITH LAYOUT TEXT

Layout text can be field labels, report titles, or any other text you want to appear on the screen or in a printed report. To add or change text on a layout, you must use the text tool. If this tool isn't selected, click once on it in the tool palette.

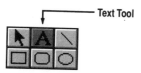

Text Tool

If you want to enter text in more than one place, double-click on the text tool when you select it. Then the text tool will remain selected after you've added text.

ADDING TEXT TO A LAYOUT

To add text to a layout, select the text tool and click once where you want to place the text on the layout. When you bring the text tool into the layout, it turns into an I-beam pointer. When you click, a dotted-line text box with a blinking insertion point appears on the layout. Type in the text you want. As you type, the text box expands.

If you want to add more than one line of text, press the Return key to start a new line.

When you're finished typing, click anywhere else on the layout to accept the text.

EDITING LAYOUT TEXT

You use standard Macintosh editing techniques to change the text in a layout. You can highlight, delete, type over, cut, copy, or paste layout text.

With the text tool selected, drag over the text that you want to change to highlight it.

Use the Delete key to delete highlighted text, or type new text to replace it. When you're finished making your changes, click anywhere else on the layout to accept them.

CHANGING THE FORMAT OF TEXT

Macintosh computers allow the use of different fonts, as well as a variety of font sizes and styles. FileMaker Pro automatically uses Helvetica as its font in layouts, but you're not stuck with it. You can change the font and format of any text object by using the commands on the Format menu. These commands let you make one change at a time. To make several format changes at once, use the Format menu's Text Format command to access the Text Format dialog box, as described in the next section.

The Format menu offers a number of pop-up menus for changing the font, size, style, alignment, line spacing, and text color.

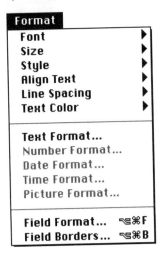

Select the object or group of objects to be formatted, pull down the Format menu, and select the appropriate command, as described in the following sections.

CHANGING THE FONT

To change the font, pull down the Format menu and drag the mouse pointer down to the Font command. The Font pop-up menu that appears includes only the fonts installed in your System file or in suitcase files accessed by your system.

Choose one of the fonts, and the selected items change to that font.

After changing a font, you may find it necessary to reposition changed objects.

CHANGING THE FONT SIZE

To change the font size, pull down the Format menu, drag the mouse pointer down to Size, and choose one of the sizes that appear in the pop-up menu.

MODIFYING
DATABASE LAYOUTS
....

CH. 4

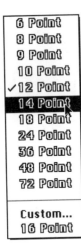

The selected items change to that size.

After changing a font's size, you may find it necessary to reposition changed objects.

CHANGING THE FONT STYLE

To change the font style, pull down the Format menu, drag the mouse pointer down to Style, and choose one of the styles that appear in the pop-up menu.

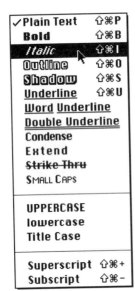

The selected items change to that style. You can repeat this step to combine as many styles as you like.

CHANGING THE TEXT ALIGNMENT

To change the text alignment, pull down the Format menu, drag the mouse pointer down to Align Text, and choose one of the alignment options that appear in the pop-up menu.

The selected items change to that alignment. You will not notice a difference in text alignment if the text you are changing completely fills the boundaries of its object.

CHANGING THE LINE SPACING

To change the line spacing, pull down the Format menu, drag the mouse pointer down to Line Spacing, and choose one of the spacing options that appear in the pop-up menu.

The selected items change to that spacing. You will not notice a difference in line spacing if the text you are changing takes up only one line.

CHANGING TEXT COLOR

To change the text color, pull down the Format menu, drag the mouse pointer down to Text Color, and choose one of the colors that appear in the pop-up menu.

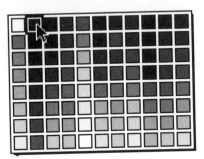

The selected items change to that color.

Only Macintosh models with 256-color capability can take advantage of the 88-color palette. Other Macintosh models will have only 8 colors available. (Of course, you need a color monitor to see the colors on your screen.)

USING THE TEXT FORMAT DIALOG BOX

The Format menu commands allow you to make all kinds of changes to the text format, but if you want to make several changes, you'll need to make multiple trips to the menu. The Text Format dialog box, however, lets you make all these changes at once.

NEW IN 2.0

Version 2.0 of FileMaker Pro adds 7 new colors, bringing the total number of available colors up to 88.

To format text using the Text Format dialog box, select the object or group of objects to be formatted. Then pull down the Format menu and choose Text Format to display the dialog box.

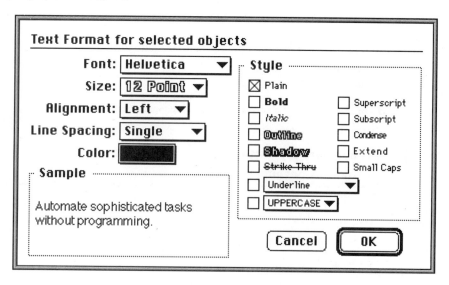

This dialog box provides pop-up menus for font, size, alignment, line spacing, and color, as well as check boxes for styles. It also provides sample text so you can see the results of your changes as you make them.

SHORTCUT

In Layout mode, double-clicking on a text object or field brings up the Text Format dialog box.

Use the pop-up menus and check boxes to change the formatting of selected objects. When you are finished making changes, click on OK. The dialog box disappears, and the selected items change to reflect your modifications.

FORMATTING NUMBERS

You can also change the way numbers look in the fields of your layout. This makes it possible to show numbers as dollars, dollars and cents, percentages, or with other special formatting.

To format numbers, select the number field or fields you want to change, pull down the Format menu, and choose Number Format. The Number Format dialog box appears.

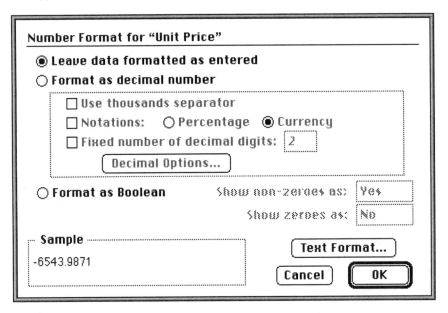

This dialog box contains a number of radio buttons, check boxes, and buttons to let you format numbers. It also includes an example of what a number looks like with the selected formatting.

Choose a number format as follows:

SHORTCUT
In Layout mode, double-clicking a number field brings up the Number Format dialog box.

- ▸ **Dollars:** To format a number field as dollars, click on the radio button for Format as Decimal Number, and then click on the check boxes for Use Thousands Separator, Notations (Currency radio button), and Fixed Number of Decimal Digits (enter a 0 or a 2).

- ▸ **Percentage:** To format a number field as a percentage, click on the radio button for Format as Decimal Number, and then click on the check boxes for Notations (Percentage radio button) and Fixed Number of Decimal Digits (enter the desired trailing decimal places).

- ▸ **Decimals:** To change the currency symbol, thousands separator, decimal point, and formatting of decimal values, click on the Decimal Options

```
┌─────────────────────────────────────────────────────────┐
│  Decimal Options for "Unit Price"                         │
│  ┌─ Symbols ─────────────────┐  ┌─ Negative Values ────┐ │
│      Currency symbol: [ $ ]        Format as: [ -1234 ▼ ]│
│   Thousands separator: [ , ]       ☐ Use color: [█████]  │
│       Decimal point: [ . ]                                │
│                                                           │
│   Currency symbol position:        [ Cancel ] [  OK  ]   │
│   ◉ Leading  ○ Trailing                                   │
└─────────────────────────────────────────────────────────┘
```

button to open the Default Decimal Options dialog box. Make appropriate changes in this dialog box and click on OK.

▸ **Text:** To make changes to the text format of the selected number field, click on the Text Format button. This brings up the Text Format dialog box described in the previous section. Make appropriate changes in this dialog box and click on OK.

When you're finished with all your number formatting changes, click on OK. The Format Number dialog box disappears.

TIP

To see the results of number formatting, switch back to Browse mode.

DRAWING LINES AND SHAPES

So far, you've learned how to use two tools from the tool palette: the pointer tool and the text tool. The other four tools on the tool palette—the line, rectangle, rounded-rectangle, and oval tools—allow you to draw graphics on your layouts. You can add graphic elements to your layout to make it more visually appealing.

NOTE

Any lines, boxes, circles, and ovals that you draw are just like any other layout objects. You can resize or reposition them as necessary.

DRAWING A LINE

Lines are commonly used to separate records on a page so you can easily see where one record ends and the next one begins. With a little imagination, you'll find a lot of other uses for lines on your layouts.

You use the line tool in the tool palette to add a line to a layout. Click once on that tool to select it.

Line Tool

If you want to draw more than one line, double-click on the line tool when you select it, so that it remains selected after you use it.

With the line tool selected, position the line tool's crossbar cursor where you want the line to begin on the layout. Press the mouse button down and drag the tool to draw a line. To draw a perfectly horizontal or vertical line, hold down the Shift key while dragging the line tool.

When the line is the right length, release the mouse button. A line, with a handle at each end, appears.

DRAWING A BOX OR CIRCLE

The rectangle, rounded-rectangle, and oval tools allow you to draw squares, rectangles, squares or rectangles with rounded edges, circles, and ovals on your layouts. Select one of the three shape tools by clicking or double-clicking it.

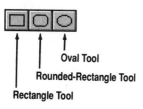
Oval Tool
Rounded-Rectangle Tool
Rectangle Tool

Position the tool's crossbar cursor where you want the object to start on your layout. When you're using the rectangle or rounded-rectangle tool, begin at any of the shape's corners. Press the mouse button down and drag diagonally.

When the object is the shape and size you have in mind, let go of the mouse button. The shape, with handles around it, appears.

SETTING THE LINE COLOR, PATTERN, AND WIDTH

You are not limited to drawing plain, black lines. FileMaker Pro allows you to change the color, pattern, and width of lines. Your changes can affect lines drawn with the line tool, as well as the ones that outline boxes and circles. You use the pen-color, pen-pattern, and line-width control buttons in the status area to set these line attributes.

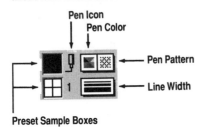

Select the line or object you want to give another color, pattern, or width, and then click on the appropriate control button.

You can use these controls to change the default settings for all lines. If none of the layout objects are selected when you adjust the pen and line-width controls, you will change the default pen settings. The default settings appear in the preset sample boxes to the left of the pen icon and line-width control button.

CHANGING LINE COLOR

To change the color of the selected line or object, click on the pen-color control button. The Pen Color pop-up menu appears, and you can select one of FileMaker Pro's 88 colors.

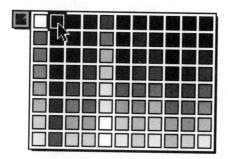

CHANGING THE PEN PATTERN

To change the pen pattern used for the selected line or object, click on the pen-pattern control button. The Pen Pattern pop-up menu appears, and you can select one of FileMaker Pro's 64 patterns. The very first pen pattern draws transparent lines and shapes.

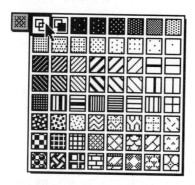

You may not notice a difference in your line when you change to some of the pen patterns unless you're changing a wide line.

CHANGING THE LINE WIDTH

To change the width of the selected line or object, click on the line-width control button. Use the Line Width pop-up menu to select one of FileMaker Pro's 11 line widths.

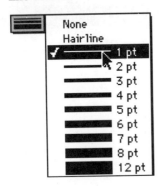

SETTING THE FILL COLOR AND PATTERN

You can also change the color and pattern that fill a shape by using the fill control buttons in the status area. These controls work exactly like the pen controls described in the previous section, except that they affect the inside of shapes rather than their outlines.

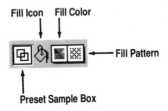

Select the shape you want to affect, and then click on the appropriate button to change its fill color or pattern.

To change the default fill settings, make sure no object is selected when you use the fill control buttons. The default settings appear in the preset sample box to the left of the fill icon.

USING THE LAYOUT MENU COMMANDS

In Layout mode, the Layout menu looks like this:

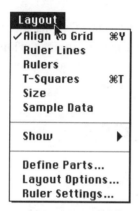

This menu offers a variety of commands and options for working with your layouts.

USING THE ALIGNMENT GRID

The Align to Grid command turns on or off FileMaker Pro's invisible, "magnetic" grid. When the grid is on, all objects that are moved or resized "snap" to it. This makes it easy to line things up, especially if your mouse hand is shaky from too much coffee!

DISPLAYING RULER LINES

NEW IN 2.0

*In previous versions of FileMaker Pro, the Ruler Lines command
was called Gridlines.*

The Ruler Lines command toggles a network of horizontal and vertical dotted
lines that correspond to the ruler units and grid spacing set through the Ruler
Settings command. Showing these lines can also make it easier to align objects.
Here's what Layout mode looks like with the ruler lines:

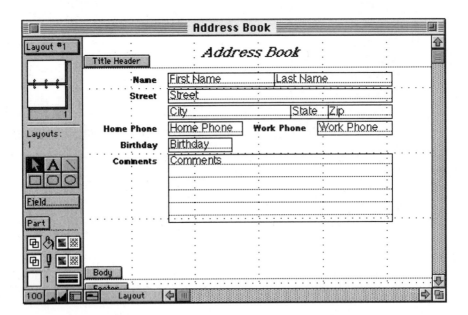

DISPLAYING THE RULERS

The Rulers command toggles the horizontal and vertical rulers on or off. The rulers' appearance depends on the units you set through the Ruler Settings command. Here's what Layout mode looks like with the rulers:

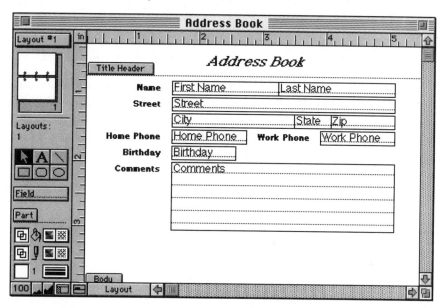

USING THE ALIGNMENT T-SQUARES

The T-Square command turns on or off the display of T-squares, which are a pair of movable horizontal and vertical lines that appear on the layout. They are magnetic (objects snap to them when moved or created) and are very useful for aligning objects. Here's what Layout mode looks like with the T-squares:

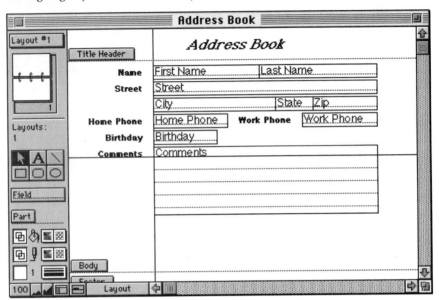

CHANGING AN OBJECT'S SIZE OR POSITION

The Size command displays the Size box, which is a floating window that shows the position and size of a selected object.

←	1.583 in
↑	2.014 in
→	5.097 in
↓	3.069 in
↔	3.514 in
↕	1.056 in

You can type new numbers into the Size box to resize or reposition selected objects.

VIEWING SAMPLE DATA

When you select the Sample Data command, each field in a layout fills with sample database data. The sample data allows you to see how your layout format will look when the fields are filled in. Here's how Layout mode appears with sample data:

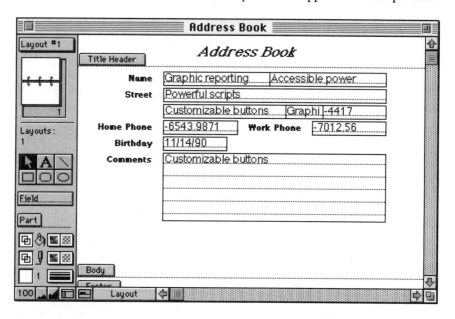

The data displayed has nothing to do with the data in your database; it's just text and numbers.

SHOWING OR HIDING LAYOUT ELEMENTS

The Show command has its own pop-up menu that lets you show or hide buttons, text boundaries, field boundaries, sliding objects, nonprinting objects, and nonprintable areas. You can use these commands to determine which of these layout aids and objects appear on the screen.

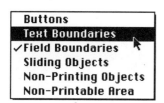

DEFINING PARTS

The Define Parts command provides another way to add or change layout parts. Selecting it displays the Define Parts dialog box. You can use this dialog box to change the order of parts or create new parts, as described in the next chapter.

SETTING LAYOUT OPTIONS

The Layout Options command allows you to change the name of a layout and to display data in multiple columns. It displays the Layout Options dialog box.

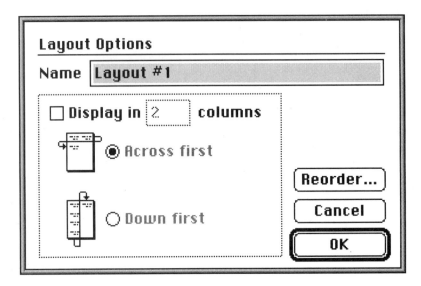

To change the name of a layout, replace the name of the layout that appears in the dialog box with the name you want to use and click on OK.

ADJUSTING THE RULER SETTINGS

The Ruler Settings command allows you to customize the ruler. It displays the Ruler Settings dialog box, in which you change the ruler units and the grid spacing.

```
┌─────────────────────────────────────────────────────────┐
│  Ruler Settings                                           │
│  ──────────────────────────────────────────────────────  │
│                                                           │
│    Units: │ Inches          ▼ │        ┌ Cancel ┐         │
│                                                           │
│    Grid Spacing: │ 6.000 │ Pixels    ▼ │   ┌  OK  ┐       │
│                                                           │
└─────────────────────────────────────────────────────────┘
```

Your choices for units include inches, centimeters, and pixels.

IN THIS CHAPTER, you learned how to manipulate layout objects. You know how to select, resize, move, format, add, and delete objects. We also covered the use of FileMaker Pro's drawing tools, which you can use to enhance your layouts with graphic elements. Finally, you learned about the Layout menu commands that help you work with layouts. You can use the techniques we covered in this chapter to create custom layouts on the screen and in printed reports.

In the next chapter, you'll learn about another important layout component: the part. Layout parts let you organize printed reports.

MODIFYING LAYOUT PARTS

IN THIS CHAPTER, you'll learn about layout parts and how to use them to organize database information in printed reports. Layout parts let you create customized headers and footers or summarize information. They also determine the position of layout objects on your printouts.

To effectively use layout parts, you need to know how to work with layout objects, which is covered in Chapter 4.

WORKING WITH LAYOUT PARTS

Each layout has one or more *parts*. A part is a section of the layout that organizes the information for printing. The way you position layout objects on parts determines where they print. The size of the part determines how much space that section of the report takes up on paper.

You must be in Layout mode to work with layout parts. Check the mode indicator at the bottom of the screen to make sure it says Layout. If not, use its pop-up menu to select Layout, choose Layout from the Select menu, or press ⌘−L to go to Layout mode.

In Layout mode parts appear separated from each other by a dotted line called the *part boundary*. You can tell which part is which by looking at the *part label* at the far left side of the part. You can add parts to a layout with the part tool, which is right beneath the field tool in the status area.

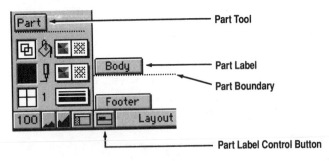

If the horizontal part labels block your view of a layout, you can click the part label control button at the bottom of the window to flip the labels up into a vertical position. Click again to flip them back.

A layout can have up to eight parts:

- **Title header:** A title header part appears at the top of the first page of a printed report. It is commonly used for report title information and introductory matter.

- **Header:** A header part appears at the top of every printed page (except the first page if a title header is defined). It is commonly used for report title information and column headings for columnar reports (see Chapter 6 for details on creating columnar reports).

- **Leading grand summary:** A *grand summary* summarizes all the information in a database or set of records that match search criteria. A leading grand summary part appears at the beginning of a report.

FOR MORE INFORMATION...

Grand summary and sub-summary parts are commonly used for report totals and subtotals. They are discussed in more detail in Chapter 10.

- **Trailing grand summary:** A trailing grand summary part appears at the end of the report.

- **Body:** The body contains the individual records of a database file. A layout contains one section of body for each record.

- **Sub-summary:** A sub-summary part summarizes information by field. A layout can include more than one sub-summary part.

- **Title footer:** A title footer part appears at the bottom of the first page. It is commonly used to show the date a report was printed.

- **Footer:** A footer part appears at the bottom of every printed page (except the first page if a title footer is defined). It is commonly used for page numbers and the date of printing.

Although your layouts can include all of these parts, most often they will include only a header, body, and footer. The header specifies the information that should

MODIFYING
LAYOUT PARTS
. . . .

CH. 5

appear at the top of each page, the body (with database fields in it) prints the contents of your database, and the footer specifies the information to appear at the bottom of the pages.

ADDING NEW PARTS

The standard layout has three parts: header, body, and footer. You can use the part tool to add other parts.

To add a part, position the mouse pointer over the part tool, press the mouse button down, and drag the tool onto the layout. The part tool itself does not move, but a part label outline and boundary appear on the layout.

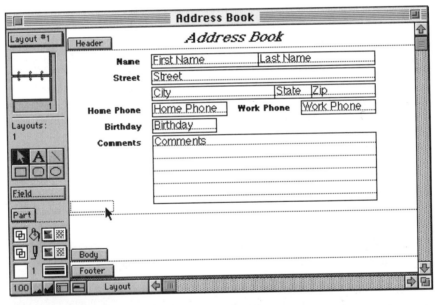

When the part label outline and boundary are where you want to place the part on your layout, release the mouse button.

After you place the part, the Part Definition dialog box appears. In this dialog box, you select the type of part you want to add. Your choices depend on where you placed the part tool. For example, if you drag the part tool above the header, the only possible part type is a title header.

Part Definition

- ⦿ **Title Header**
- ○ Header
- ○ **Leading Grand Summary**
- ○ Body
- ○ Sub-Summary when sorted by:
- ○ Trailing Grand Summary
- ○ Footer
- ○ Title Footer

First Name
Last Name
Street
City
State
Zip
Home Phone
Work Phone

- ☐ Page break before each occurrence
- ☐ Page break after every [1] occurrences
- ☐ **Restart page numbers after each occurrence**
- ☐ Allow part to break across page boundaries
  - ☐ Discard remainder of part before new page

[Cancel]

[**OK**]

Select the part you want by clicking on the radio button beside it, and then click on OK. The part appears on your layout. You can now add fields, text, or graphics to it, as appropriate.

FOR MORE INFORMATION...

The Part Definition dialog box also has options for setting page breaks. These options are discussed in Chapter 10.

ADDING PAGE NUMBERS, DATES, OR TIMES

When you want each page of a report to appear with a page number or the date or time of printing, place it in a header or footer part. However, if you simply type in a page number on your layout, the same page number will appear on each page. And if you type in a date or time, that date or time will always appear on the report, no matter when the report is printed.

Instead of typing in the information, you use FileMaker Pro's special codes for the page number, date, and time. Use the text tool to enter one or more of these codes into a header or footer:

- To enter the page number, type in two pound signs (##). If you want the word *Page* to precede the page number, you can type that in as well: *Page ##*.

- To have the current date appear on the layout, type in two slashes (*//*). If you want the word *Revised* or *Printed* to precede the date, you can type that in as well: *Revised //*.

- To have the current time appear on the layout, type in two colons (*::*). If you want the words *Print Time* to precede the time, you can type that in as well: *Print Time ::*.

When you view your database in Preview mode or print it, these codes are replaced with the information they represent.

RESIZING PARTS

A part's size determines the amount of space it takes up on paper when it is printed. A part is measured from the bottom boundary of the part above it to its bottom boundary. If a part is too small, you may not be able to fit all the objects you need in it. If a part is too big, your printouts may have excess white space.

You can resize a part in the same way that you resize other layout objects. Position the pointer tool over the bottom boundary of a part to be resized and press the mouse button. Drag the boundary down to make the part larger, or up to make the part smaller.

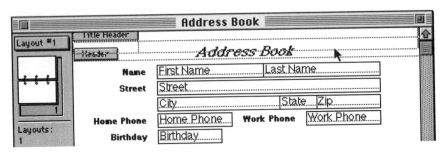

When the bottom boundary appears to be in the right place, release the mouse button. The part size changes, and all the parts below it shift accordingly.

REMOVING PARTS

When you no longer need a part, you can remove it. Click once on the part label for the part you want to delete.

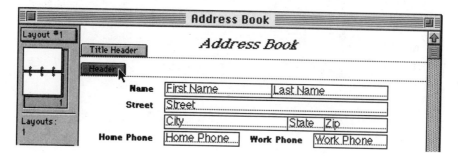

Press the Delete key. If the part you want to delete contains objects, you will see this warning dialog box:

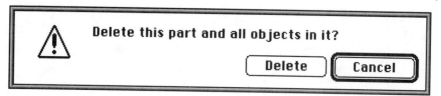

WARNING

Use care when deleting a part that contains fields, especially the body. You could end up with a report that has no information in it!

If you're sure you want to delete the part and the objects in it, click on the Delete button. FileMaker Pro removes the part from the layout.

IN THIS CHAPTER, you learned how to add, resize, and delete layout parts. We also covered how to use a header or footer to display a report's page numbers and the date and time of printing. Working with parts makes it possible to determine the exact position of layout objects to fully customize printed reports.

In the next chapter, you'll learn how to create new layouts from scratch. We'll discuss the different types of layouts FileMaker Pro offers and how to create columnar reports, mailing labels, and other useful layouts for reports and printouts.

CREATING NEW LAYOUTS

FILEMAKER PRO OFFERS a variety of layout types that let you create custom documents, such as columnar reports, mailing labels, and data-entry forms. In this chapter, you'll learn how to create several new layouts—at least one of each type—from scratch.

After you've created a layout, you can modify it by using the techniques covered in Chapter 4.

WORKING WITH LAYOUT TYPES

So far, we've been working with the standard layout. However, FileMaker Pro offers seven different types of layouts:

▸ **Standard layout:** Each field in the body of a standard layout is in the order it appears in the Define Fields dialog box. It contains one field per line, and the field name appears to the left of the field. The layout also includes a header and a footer. A standard layout is useful for data entry, as well as for creating find requests. (Find requests are search criteria definitions, as explained in Chapter 7.)

FOR MORE INFORMATION...
By adding summary fields and summary parts to a columnar report, you can create subtotals and grand totals for financial reports. Summary fields and summary parts are discussed in Chapter 10.

▸ **Columnar report layout:** Each field in the body of a columnar report layout is in one or more lines. You select which fields to include and specify their order. Each field name appears in the header above the field. In Browse mode or when printed, the fields appear in columns. The layout also includes a footer. Columnar reports are useful for showing tabular information.

▸ **Extended columnar report layout:** This layout is similar to a regular columnar report layout. However, instead of wrapping fields to a second line when they don't fit on the page, the extended columnar report layout places all the fields on one line in the body. This layout is especially useful when you have more fields than would normally fit on one line of the first page.

The extended columnar report layout is a new type.

- **Single page form layout:** With this layout, you can take up a full page or more than one page. Each field in the body of a single page form layout is in the order it appears in the Define Fields dialog box. It contains one field per line, and the field name appears to the left of the field. The layout does not include a header or footer. This layout is useful when you want each record to appear on its own page or group of pages.

- **Label layout:** In a label layout, the selected fields appear in the body, one per line, in the order you specify. The size of the body depends on the type of printer and labels you are using. The font size of the fields is reduced to fit more fields in the smaller space. Field names are not included. Both a header and footer are included, but they are usually used for spacing considerations and rarely for text. Use this layout to create any kind of label.

- **Envelope layout:** In an envelope layout, the selected fields appear in the body, one per line, in the order you specify. Additional spacing is automatically added to position the fields properly for an envelope address. Field names and a footer are not included. A header is included to provide proper spacing for center-fed envelopes. Use this layout to print addresses or other information on business envelopes.

- **Blank:** A blank layout is simply that: a blank layout, without fields or field names. A header and footer are included, but they are also blank. You can add and position text, graphics, fields, and parts with the layout tools in the status area. Blank layouts are useful for form letters, on-screen instructions, and menus.

**CREATING
NEW LAYOUTS**

. . . .

CH. 6

CREATING A LAYOUT

To create a new layout, you must be in Layout mode. Use the Select menu, Mode pop-up menu, or ⌘-L key combination to switch to Layout mode. You can create a new layout based on any of FileMaker Pro's predefined layouts.

To create a new layout, select New Layout from the Edit menu. The New Layout dialog box appears.

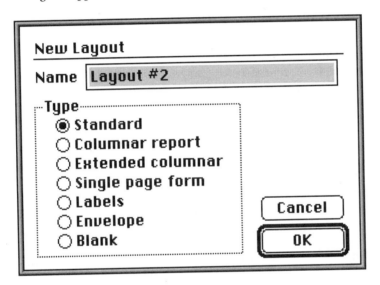

SHORTCUT

In Layout mode, press the ⌘-N key combination to create a new layout.

In the Name edit box, type in a name for the new layout. Then click on the radio button for the type of layout you want to create and click on OK.

Depending on the layout type, you may see the new layout immediately, or you may need to provide more information before the layout appears. You can modify your newly created layout by using the techniques described in Chapters 4 and 5.

CREATING A NEW STANDARD LAYOUT

A standard layout is one of the easiest to create. After you type in a name for the new layout, make sure the radio button for Standard is selected, and click on OK, the new layout appears.

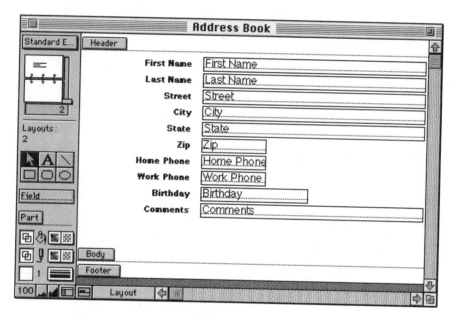

CREATING A COLUMNAR REPORT

One of the features of a columnar report is that you can specify the fields to include and the order in which to include them. After you type in a name for the new layout in the New Layout dialog box, click on the radio button for Columnar report, and then click on OK.

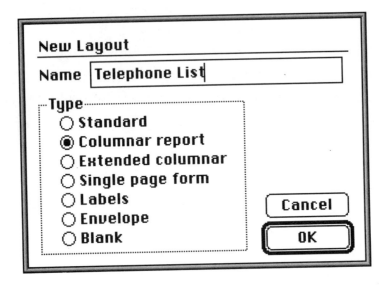

The Set Field Order dialog box appears. On the left side of the dialog box is the Field List window, which shows all the fields in the current database. On the right side of the dialog box is the Field Order window, which will contain the fields to include in the layout.

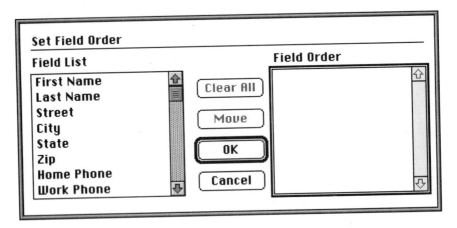

Select the fields to include in the order you want them to appear. To select a field for inclusion, click once on the field name in the Field List window and click on the Move button to add it to the Field Order window. You can also select a field to include by double-clicking on its name in the Field List window to copy it to the Field Order window.

Continue to select each field you want to include. If necessary, use the Clear All or Clear button to clear all or one of the entries in the Field Order dialog box.

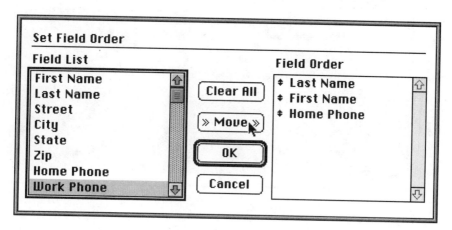

NEW IN 2.0

You can reorder fields in the Field Order window. Drag the double-arrow icon to the left of a field to move that field up or down.

When all the fields you want to include appear in the Field Order window, click on OK. The new layout appears.

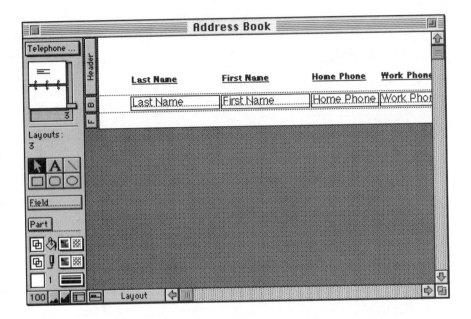

CREATING AN EXTENDED COLUMNAR REPORT

. . . .

WARNING
Fields and other layout objects that extend beyond a page bound-
ary will not print.

You create an extended columnar report layout in the same way that you create a
new columnar report layout. Use this type of layout when you want to include
many fields. However, if you include more than five or six fields, the layout may

extend over the edge of the page boundary, as in this example:

You will need to modify the layout to squeeze all the fields within the page boundaries if you want them to print.

CREATING A SINGLE PAGE FORM

As when you create a new standard layout, your new single page form layout appears after you type a name, click on the radio button for a single page form layout, and click on OK in the New Layout dialog box.

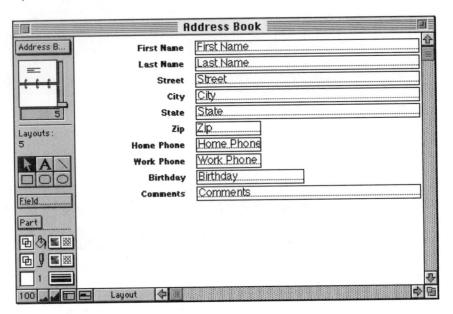

CREATING MAILING LABELS

Mailing labels are probably the toughest of all layouts to get just right. It isn't enough for them to just look good on paper; each label must fit into its allotted space on the label forms.

You can create a label layout by using one of FileMaker Pro's Avery templates, or without using a template.

NEW IN 2.0

You can take advantage of preset templates for many Avery label sizes. (Avery is a major manufacturer of labels.) These templates greatly simplify the creation of standard labels.

USING THE AVERY TEMPLATES

If you use standard format labels with your computer and printer, label-making will be a breeze. Simply make a note of the Avery label number (or Avery equivalent, if you are using another maker's labels) before you begin.

When you click on the radio button for Labels and then click on OK in the New Layout dialog box, the Label Setup dialog box appears.

In this dialog box, you give FileMaker Pro information about the labels you will use.

Label Setup

⦿ **Use label measurements for** ✓ Avery 4143
　　　　　　　　　　　　　　　　　　 Avery 4144
○ **Use custom measurements:**　 Avery 4603
　　　　　　　　　　　　　　　　　　 Avery 4605
　　　　　　　　　　　　　　　　　　 Avery 4609
　　　　　　　　　　　　　　　　　　 Avery 4610
　　　　　　　　　　　　　　　　　　 Avery 4611
　　　　　　　　　　　　　　　　　　 Avery 5095
　　　　　　　　　　　　　　　　　　 Avery 5096
　　　　　　　　　　　　　　　　　　 Avery 5097
　　　　　　　　　　　　　　　　　　 Avery 5160/5260
　　　　　　　　　　　　　　　　　　 Avery 5161/5261
　　　　　　　　　　　　　　　　　　 Avery 5162/5262
　　　　　　　　　　　　　　　　　　 Avery 5163/5263
　　　　　　　　　　　　　　　　　　 Avery 5164

**CREATING
NEW LAYOUTS**

. . . .

CH. 6

Make sure the radio button for the top option, Use Label Measurements For, is selected, and use that option's pop-up menu to select the label number of the labels you will use.

Click on OK, and the Set Field Order dialog box appears.

. . . .

NEW IN 2.0

The Label Setup dialog box now offers two ways to provide label information.

This dialog box works the same as the one you use to select the fields to include in a columnar report layout. Choose the fields in the order you want them to appear by double-clicking on the name in the Field List window, or by clicking once on the name and once on the Move button. When all the fields you want to include appear in the Field Order window, click on OK. The label layout appears.

. . . .

NOTE

Use the Clear All or Clear button to clear entries in the Field Order window.

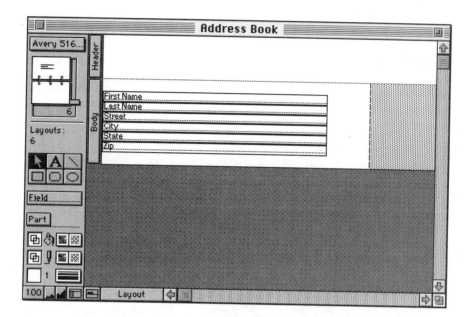

If you're creating mailing labels, you'll need to resize and reposition fields to make them look like labels. For example, if City, State, and Zip are three separate fields, they'll appear on three separate lines unless you change them. Use the techniques described in Chapter 4 to make the necessary modifications. For example, you could arrange the fields this way:

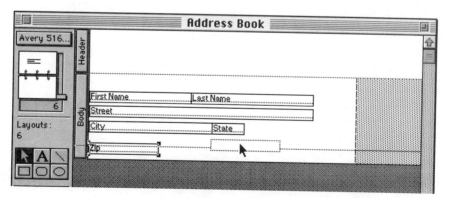

CREATING
NEW LAYOUTS
. . . .

CH. 6

You can enlarge your view of a label layout by using the zoom controls at the bottom of the window, as described in Chapter 1. Click once on the icon with the larger mountains to increase the size to 200 percent.

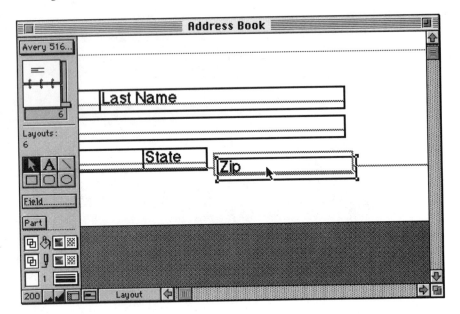

Click once on the icon with the smaller mountains to return to normal size.

In Browse mode, you'll notice gaps between the contents of fields in your label layout.

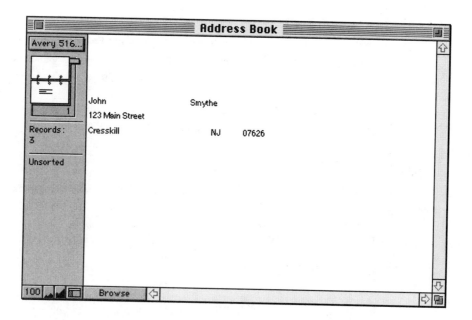

In Preview mode (and the printout), however, those gaps are closed up.

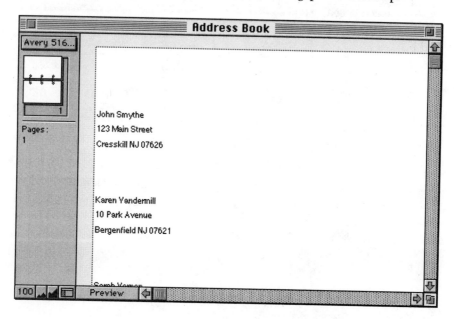

CREATING LABELS WITHOUT TEMPLATES

You can create your own custom label layouts by selecting the Labels radio button in the New Layout dialog box, and then choosing the Use Custom Measurements option (the bottom radio button) in the Label Setup dialog box.

In the appropriate edit boxes, enter the number of labels across the page, the width of each label, and the height of each label. When specifying the width and height of labels, enter measurements in inches and include any space between labels.

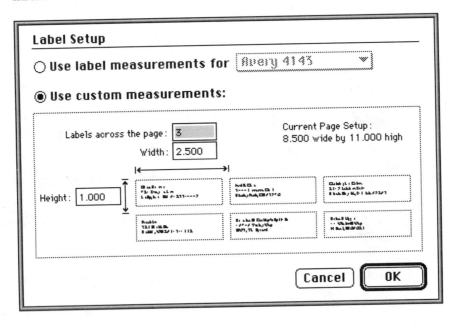

Click on OK, and then use the Set Field Order dialog box to select the fields to include in the layout, as described earlier in the chapter. Click on OK, and the new layout appears. You can modify the layout by using the techniques described in Chapter 4.

CREATING AN ENVELOPE LAYOUT

An envelope layout lets you address envelopes without worrying about labels. You can add a return address, special message, and graphics to an envelope layout.

After you select the Envelope radio button in the New Layout dialog box and click on OK, the Set Field Order dialog box appears. Select the fields to include in the order you want them to appear, as described earlier in the chapter, and then click on OK. The new layout appears.

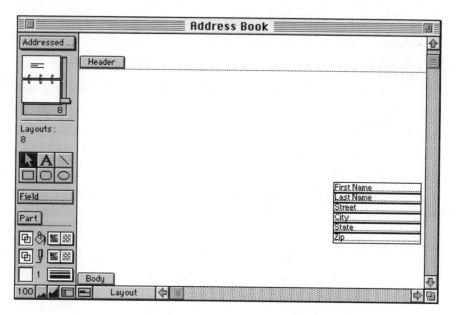

Modify the layout as necessary using the techniques covered in Chapter 4. If you want to include a return address, be sure to enter it in the body of the layout:

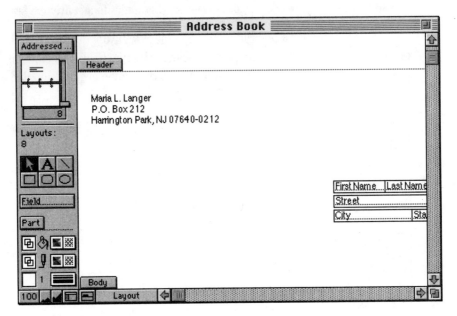

CREATING A BLANK LAYOUT

Since it doesn't contain any fields, creating a blank layout is simple. After you choose the radio button for Blank and click on OK in the New Layout dialog box, the new layout appears.

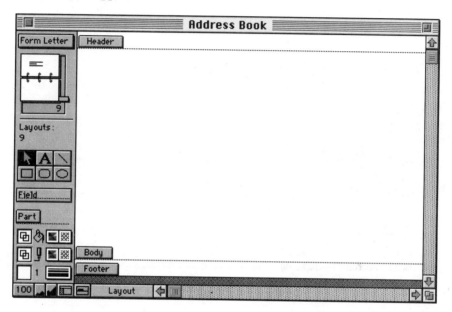

Add text, fields, graphics, and parts using the techniques described in Chapters 4 and 5. Here's an example of a form letter created with a blank layout:

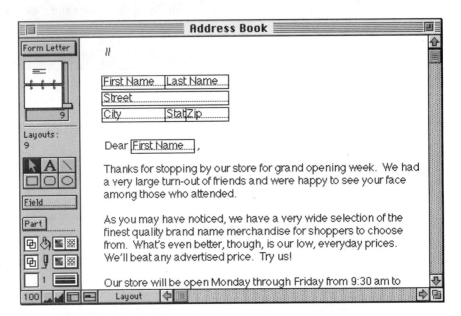

MOVING FROM LAYOUT TO LAYOUT

After you have more than one layout, you will want to switch from one to another. Layouts are always in the order they were created. You can use the book or the Layout menu to move among your layouts.

NOTE

Using the book to move among layouts is similar to using it to move to other database records. See Chapter 3 for details.

In Layout mode, when you have more than one layout, the book near the top of the status area has lines on the top page, the bottom page, or both pages. With the book, you can move from layout to layout by using one of these three methods:

▶ Click on a page of the book with lines on it to scroll up or down through the layouts.

▶ Drag the bookmark on the book up or down. When the layout number at the bottom of the book is the one you want to see, release the bookmark.

▶ Click on the layout number at the bottom of the book, type the number of the layout you want to see, and press Return.

The Layout pop-up menu at the very top of the status area always shows the name of the current layout. You can click on this menu and select another layout from the options that appear.

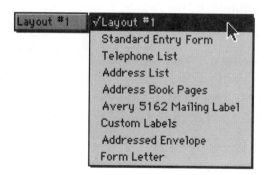

DUPLICATING A LAYOUT

As you work with FileMaker Pro, you may find instances where one layout is almost exactly the same as another you need to create. Rather than create the new
layout from scratch, you can duplicate the existing layout and then modify the
copy.

With the layout you want to duplicate on your screen, select Duplicate Layout from
the Edit menu. The new layout that appears is identical to the one you duplicated.
FileMaker Pro puts the word *Copy* after the old layout name to name the duplicate.

Make changes as appropriate to customize this new layout. To change the name
of the layout, choose the Layout Options command on the Layout menu and enter
a new name in the Layout Options dialog box, as described in Chapter 4.

DELETING A LAYOUT

When you no longer need a layout, you can remove it. With the layout you want to
delete on your screen, select Delete Layout from the Edit menu. You see this warning dialog box:

WARNING

Deleting a layout cannot be undone, so be sure you really want to delete it before you click on the Delete button.

If you're sure you want to delete the layout, click on the Delete button. The layout is removed from the file.

IN THIS CHAPTER, you learned about the seven types of layouts FileMaker Pro offers and what purposes they can serve. We covered the procedures for creating each type of layout. You also learned how to move from layout to layout, duplicate layouts, and delete layouts.

In the next chapter, you'll learn how to use FileMaker's Find mode to search for records. Finding specific records makes it possible to gather the information you need and create custom reports.

FINDING INFORMATION

AFTER YOU'VE GOT a database full of records, browsing through them one at a time to find specific records can be time-consuming. Fortunately, FileMaker Pro's Find command can locate information for you.

So far, we've worked in Browse and Layout modes. You saw that Browse mode lets you enter and edit database contents, and Layout mode lets you customize the way your database looks on the screen and on paper. In Find mode, you can search for records based on the criteria you provide. This chapter describes how to find information quickly and easily.

SWITCHING TO FIND MODE

To find records with FileMaker Pro, you must create one or more *find requests*. A find request is a description of what you want to find. The description is stated as *criteria*, which are the pieces of information FileMaker should locate.

You create find requests in FileMaker Pro's Find mode. You can switch to Find mode by choosing Find from the Select menu or by selecting Find from the Mode pop-up menu at the bottom of the FileMaker Pro window.

SHORTCUT
From any mode, press the ⌘–F key combination to switch to Find mode.

When you switch to Find mode, the FileMaker Pro window displays a blank record form in whatever layout you were in before you changed modes. The window may look something like this:

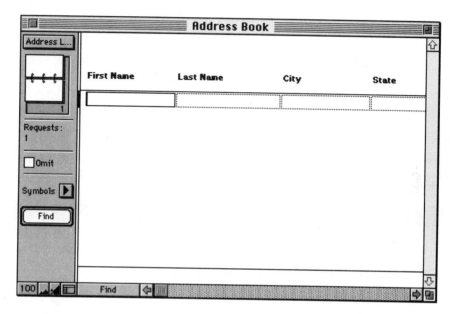

The status area now contains tools for finding records. If the status area does not appear when you switch to Find mode, click on the status area control button at the bottom of the document window to display it.

NEW IN 2.0

The appearance of the status area in Find mode is different, but it works much the same way.

The area immediately beneath the book no longer shows the number of records. Instead, it shows the number of find requests. You can use the book to move from one request to another in the same way that you use it to move among your records in Browse mode (see Chapter 3).

Three status area items don't appear in Browse or Layout mode:

▸ **Omit check box:** This check box tells FileMaker Pro to show all records *except* those that match the criteria you enter.

▸ **Symbols pop-up menu:** This pop-up menu lists the symbols that you can use in your criteria. You can select the symbols from the menu or simply type them in from the keyboard.

▸ **Find button:** When you're finished creating your find request, clicking on this button instructs FileMaker Pro to look for matches for the criteria you specified.

CREATING FIND REQUESTS

To create a find request, you enter each part of the criteria in the field in which it is likely to be met, and FileMaker Pro looks through *all* the records in the database for matches. If the current layout does not include a field you need to enter a criterion in, use the Layout pop-up menu to select a layout that does.

For example, if you want to find people in your address book database based on their city, you would enter the name of the city in the City field. This tells File-Maker Pro what to look for as well as where to look for it. You must enter the information just the way it appears and in the field in which it is stored. If you put the criteria in the wrong fields, FileMaker probably won't find the information you had in mind, or it may not find anything at all.

FINDING RECORDS THAT MATCH ONE CRITERION

The most basic type of find request uses one criterion. Switch to Find mode by using one of the techniques described at the beginning of the chapter, type the criterion in the appropriate field, and click on the Find button.

For example, to search an address book database for everyone who lives in the state of California, press ⌘-F to switch to Find mode and type **CA** in the State field.

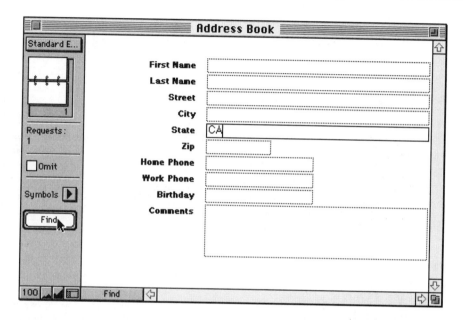

In this example, you would not enter the criterion as *California*, because the common two-letter abbreviation, *CA*, is used in the database. When you click on the Find button, FileMaker Pro finds all records with CA in the State field.

NARROWING YOUR SEARCH: MATCHING MULTIPLE CRITERIA

You may need to find records based on two or more criteria. Just place the information that you want to match in the appropriate fields. When you include multiple criteria in the same find request, FileMaker Pro finds only the records that match *all* of them.

FINDING INFORMATION
. . . .

CH. 7

For example, to search an address book database for people who live in New York *and* have a home phone number area code of 212, enter NY in the State field and 212 in the Home Phone field.

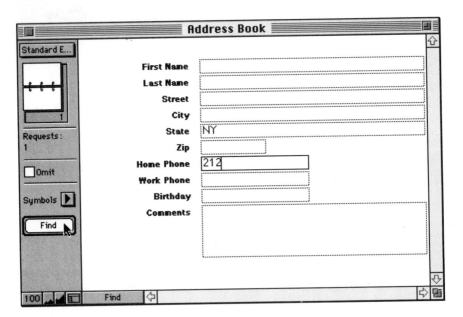

When you click on the Find button, FileMaker Pro finds just those records that have NY in the State field as well as 212 in the Home Phone field.

As this example shows, FileMaker Pro can match the beginning characters in an entry. This works only in text fields, however. FileMaker Pro always looks for exact matches in number fields. In the example, the phone number field is a text field, so entering *212* finds that area code. If a phone number field is a number field, you would need to type in a whole phone number as the criterion to get a match.

TIP

You can always change a number field to a text field if the field is not used in a calculation. After it's a text field, you can enter the beginning numbers as search criteria.

BROADENING YOUR SEARCH: USING MULTIPLE FIND REQUESTS

You can also use multiple find requests to search a database. When you create more than one find request, FileMaker Pro finds records that match *any* of them.

Switch to Find mode and create your first find request (don't click on the Find button). Then select New Request from the Edit menu. FileMaker Pro presents another blank find request form. Fill in your next set of criteria. You can continue to create new find requests to widen the scope of the search. When you are finished defining requests, click on Find. FileMaker Pro matches the records that meet any of the sets of criteria.

SHORTCUT

In Find mode, press the ⌘-D key combination to duplicate a find request.

For example, to search an address book database for people who live in New York State *or* New Jersey, switch to Find mode and type NY in the State field. Then press ⌘-N to create a new request. The book shows that you're viewing request 2, and the area beneath the book shows that there are 2 requests.

Requests: 2

In the State field, type in NJ. Then click on the Find button. FileMaker Pro finds all records with NY *or* NJ in the State field.

You are not limited to two find requests. You can create as many as you need to find particular records. Remember, you can use the book to move from request to request.

You can also duplicate requests to make it easier to prepare similar find requests. To make a copy of a request, use the Duplicate Request command on the Edit menu.

TIP

In Find mode, the ⌘–D key combination to duplicate a find request.

Each find request can have multiple criteria. So you could, for example, find people living in New York who have last names beginning with *L* as well as people living in San Diego with first names beginning with *P*. The possibilities are endless. Until you're confident about using multiple criteria and multiple find requests, however, be sure to check the records that FileMaker Pro found to make certain they are the ones you expected.

FINDING RECORDS THAT DON'T MATCH CRITERIA

The Omit check box in the status area lets you find records that don't match the find request. You enter criteria in the appropriate fields, check Omit, and then click on Find. FileMaker Pro finds all the records *except* those that match the criteria.

For example, to search an address book database for people who live in any state except California, type CA in the State field, and then click on the Omit check box to turn it on.

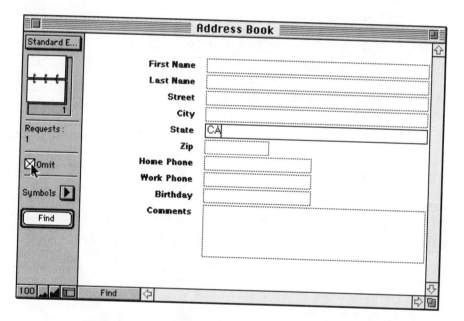

Click on the Find button. FileMaker Pro finds all records with anything but CA in the State field.

USING SPECIAL SYMBOLS TO FIND RECORDS

You can use special symbols in your find requests to locate certain records. The symbols are listed on the Symbols pop-up menu.

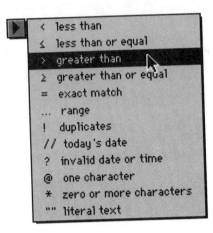

NEW IN 2.0

*The Symbols pop-up menu offers several new symbols: ? (invalid date or time), @ (any single character), * (zero or more characters), and "" (literal text).*

The symbols work as follows:

▶ **< (Less than):** To use the less than symbol, enter it in a find request field and then type in a value. For example, entering *<1000* in a number field instructs FileMaker to search for records with values less than 1000 in that particular field. You can also use this symbol in date, time, calculation, and even text fields. For example, entering *<M* in a text field finds all records with words that start with letters before *M* in that field.

- ≤ **(Less than or equal):** The less than or equal to symbol works like the less than symbol, but it also looks for values that match the one entered after the symbol.

- > **(Greater than):** The greater than symbol works like the less than symbol, but it looks for values greater than the one entered after the symbol.

- ≥ **(Greater than or equal):** The greater than or equal to symbol works like the greater than symbol, but it also looks for values that match the one entered after the symbol.

- = **(Exact match):** The exact match symbol finds exactly what you enter after it. For example, if your database includes someone named Chris and someone named Christopher, entering *Chris* in the appropriate field of a find request would find both. If you want to find only Chris and not Christopher, enter *=Chris*. You don't need to use this symbol in number, date, and time fields, because FileMaker Pro always looks for exact matches in those types of fields.

TIP

To find empty fields, enter the exact match symbol (=) by itself in the appropriate field of a find request and click on Find.

- ... **(Range):** Use the range symbol between starting and ending values for a range. For example, if you want to find values between 500 and 5000 in a number field, enter *500...5000* in that field. This symbol also works in text, date, time, and calculation fields.

- ! **(Duplicates):** The duplicates symbol finds all records that do not have unique values in that field. This symbol works in text, number, date, time, and calculation fields.

- **// (Today's date):** Entering the today's date symbol in a date field finds all records with the current date in the field.

- **? (Invalid date or time):** Entering the invalid date or time symbol in a date or time field finds records with invalid information in the field.

- **@ (One character):** Use the one character wildcard symbol when you want to match any one character in a text field. For example, say you want to find someone with a last name of Jenson or Jensen—you can't remember how he spells it. In the appropriate field of a find request, enter *Jens@n*. FileMaker Pro substitutes any single character for the @ and looks for matches.

- *** (Zero or more characters):** The zero or more characters wildcard symbol matches any characters in a text field. For example, if you want to find all records with a *TH* anywhere in the last name field, enter **th** in the field. FileMaker Pro substitutes either no characters or any group of characters for the * and looks for matches. Thus, it will find entries such as Thomas, Anther, and Booth.

- **"" (Literal text):** The literal text symbol matches exactly any text you place within the quotation marks. This symbol is especially useful if you want to find several words that would appear together in a long text field, such as "on backorder" or "payment due."

WORKING WITH THE FOUND SET

After you click on the Find button to initiate a search, FileMaker Pro finds the records that match your field request and displays them in Browse mode. All the other records in the database are temporarily hidden. The status area summarizes the results of a find request by showing the total number of records and the number of records found.

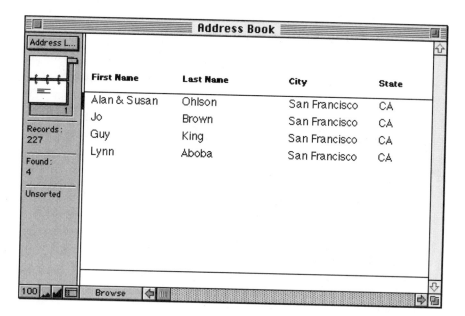

The group of records found as a result of a find request is called the *found set*. For example, if you instruct FileMaker Pro to find all the people in your address book database who live in San Francisco, the found set will include only those records containing San Francisco in the City field.

You can use the book to scroll through the records in the found set. Using the book to scroll through records is described in Chapter 3.

You can work with the found set in several ways:

- Sort the found set without affecting the other records in the database (see Chapter 8).

- Switch to a different layout, and the same found set appears (see Chapter 6).

- Print the found set (see Chapter 9).

FINDING INFORMATION
. . . .

CH. 7

By using these functions—sorting, switching to another layout, and printing—you can create a custom report that includes only the records that match your criteria, in the layout you choose.

For example, you could search an address book database to find all the people who live in the 908 area code, sort them by last name, and display them as mailing labels:

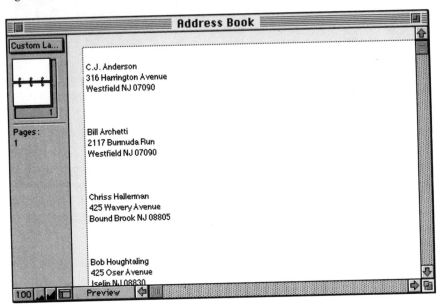

FINDING ALL RECORDS

As you've seen, after using the Find command, only the found set appears. The rest of the records in the database are temporarily hidden.

When you're finished working with the found set and want to work with the rest of the records in the database, you need to instruct FileMaker Pro to find all the records. Select the Find All command on the Select menu, and all the records reappear.

SHORTCUT

In any mode, the ⌘-J key combination finds all records.

THIS CHAPTER DESCRIBED Find mode and how to use it to find information based on any criteria you specify. You learned how to create find requests with single and multiple criteria. You also saw how to use the Omit check box and special symbols to locate particular records.

In the next chapter, you'll see how FileMaker Pro lets you sort the records in an entire database or just in the found set. This makes it easier to find specific information in printed reports and to summarize information.

SORTING RECORDS

AS YOU ADD records to your database, FileMaker Pro stores them at the end of the database file. As a result, the records in your database are stored in the order you enter them. But this isn't always the order you want to view them in on screen or in printed reports.

FileMaker Pro provides a Sort command that lets you sort records based on one or more fields. You can use the command to arrange all the records in your database or just those in the found set (the records located by a find request, as described in Chapter 7). As you will learn in this chapter, sorting allows you to put any collection of records into whatever order you like.

THE FILEMAKER PRO SORT CONDITIONS

FileMaker Pro has three sort conditions: unsorted, sorted, and semi-sorted. In Browse mode, you can see the current sort condition notation in the status area:

So far, you've seen only the word *Unsorted* in the status area. Until you sort the records of a database, they are unsorted; that is, they are in the order you entered them. After you sort records, the status area notation changes to *Sorted*. These two conditions are straightforward and easy to understand.

The semi-sorted condition is another story. When the status area shows the word *Semi-sorted*, it means that the database was sorted but additional records were added after the sort. Strictly speaking, the records are no longer sorted, but they can't be considered unsorted either, so FileMaker Pro describes their sort condition as semi-sorted.

SPECIFYING THE SORT ORDER

When you are ready to sort the records in a database or found set, select the Sort command from the Select menu. The Sort dialog box appears.

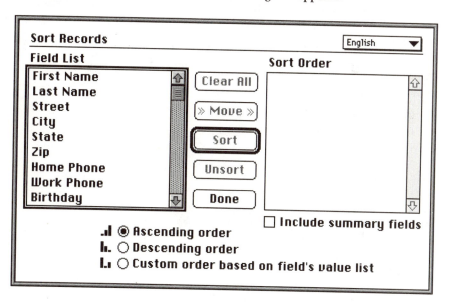

In this dialog box, you define the order in which you want to sort the records.

SHORTCUT
In any mode, the ⌘–S key combination accesses the Sort dialog box.

Let's take a look at the parts of this dialog box:

▶ **Field List window:** This window lists all the fields in your database, in the same order they appear in the Define Fields dialog box (see Chapter 2).

▶ **Sort Order window:** This window displays the current sort order. If you have never sorted records in your database, it will be empty. If you have sorted records, it will display the last sort order you created.

▶ **Sort Language pop-up menu:** This pop-up menu is in the upper-right corner of the dialog box. Because alphabetical order may be different from one country to another, FileMaker Pro lets you specify which language you want to use to sort. English is the default selection for versions of FileMaker Pro sold in the United States. You can choose from 15 languages.

NEW IN 2.0

The Language pop-up menu no longer appears as an icon representing a pair of globes, but it works the same way.

▸ **Sort order radio buttons**: The Ascending Order and Descending Order radio buttons let you select whether you want to sort a specific field in ascending (first to last), or descending (last to first) order. If a selected field has a value list that you created as part of the field definition (see Chapter 11), the Custom Order radio button will also be available.

▸ **Action buttons:** These buttons help you create the sort order (Clear All and Move/Clear), sort based on the sort order (Sort), unsort records (Unsort), and dismiss the dialog box without sorting (Done).

▸ **Include Summary Fields check box:** Placing a check in this check box includes summary fields in the Field List window.

You specify the sort order by moving fields from the Field List window to the Sort Order window. Click on the name of the field you want to sort by in the Field List window. If necessary, click on the Ascending Order, Descending Order, or Custom Order radio button to change the way the field is sorted.

Click on the Move button, and the field name appears in the Sort Order window. If you make a mistake, you can click on the field in the Sort Order window and click on the Clear button to remove the selected field.

SHORTCUT

You can double-click on a field name in the Field List window to select it and move it to the Sort Order window.

PERFORMING A SINGLE-LEVEL SORT

A single-level sort sorts by one field. Access the Sort dialog box by selecting Sort from the Select menu or by pressing ⌘-S. If necessary, click on the Clear All button to remove any undesired fields listed in the Sort Order window.

In the Field List window, select the field you want to sort by and move it to the Sort Order window, as described in the previous section.

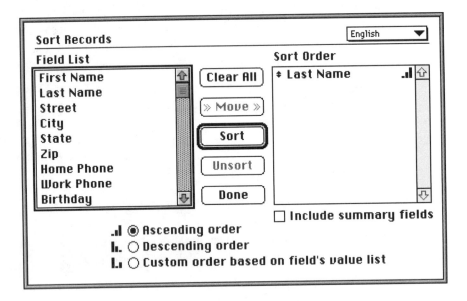

Click on the Sort button. FileMaker Pro sorts the records in the database or found set.

If you are sorting a database with many records, FileMaker Pro may display a progress dialog box to show you how it's doing. When it's finished sorting the records, it returns you to the mode you were in before you accessed the Sort dialog box. Here's an example of an address book database sorted by the Last Name field in ascending order:

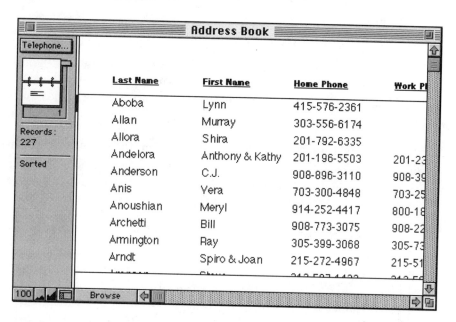

To see the records sorted, you must be in Browse or Preview mode.

TIP

The best way to view sorted records is in a layout that shows more than one record at a time. You can use the Layout pop-up menu above the book to switch to another layout. The records remain sorted in any layout.

PERFORMING A MULTIPLE-LEVEL SORT

A single-level sort is sufficient for many sorting situations. In fact, it may be the only kind of sorting you do. However, when you're sorting by a field that contains many duplicate values, you may want to specify another field to arrange the records within the main order. For example, if you're sorting an address book

SORTING RECORDS
. . . .

CH. 8

database by a State field and you have more than one record for each state, you can tell FileMaker Pro to sort the records within each state by the City or Last Name field.

To arrange records by more than one field, you perform a multiple-level sort. In the Sort dialog box, click on the name of the first field you want to sort by, change the sort order for that field if necessary, and then click on the Move button. Then click on the name of the second field you want to sort by in the Field List window and move it into the Sort Order window.

Continue to add as many fields as you like to the Sort Order window. If you need to change their order in the Sort Order window, use the Clear All button to erase all the entries and begin selecting fields again. When you're finished, the Sort Order window might look something like this:

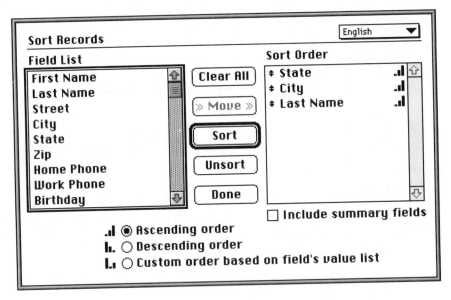

NEW IN 2.0

You can change the order of fields listed in the Sort Order window without starting over. Use the double-arrow icon to the left of each field name to drag it up or down in the field order.

Click on the Sort button. FileMaker Pro sorts the records by the first field. When it finds more than one record with the same value in that field, it sorts those records by the second field. If it finds more than one record with the same value in both fields, it sorts by the third field, and so on until all the records are in the order you specified. An address book database sorted by the State, City, then Last Name fields might look something like this:

	Address Book			
Address L...	**First Name**	**Last Name**	**City**	**State**
	Janice	Wirthlin	Huntsville	AL
	Dr.	Steve	Casa Grande	AZ
Records: 227	Cheryl	Crawford	Phoenix	AZ
	Fred & Cheri	Gagne	Phoenix	AZ
Sorted	Mitch	LaPage	Tubac	AZ
	George &	Johnson	Alameda	CA
	Marguerite	Steiner	Alameda	CA
	Zeff	Dilian	Aptos	CA
	Alan	Engst	Berkeley	CA
	Paul, Mary, &	Halloran	Berkeley	CA

CH. 8

UNSORTING RECORDS

You can also return records to their unsorted order. After you unsort the records, they will once again be in the order in which they were created.

To unsort records, select the Sort command from the Select menu (or press ⌘–S), and then click on the Unsort button. FileMaker Pro returns the records to their normal order.

IN THIS CHAPTER, you learned about FileMaker Pro's three sort conditions: unsorted, sorted, and semi-sorted. We covered both single-level and multiple-level sorts. You also learned how to unsort records to return them to FileMaker Pro's normal order.

The next chapter describes how to get your information on paper. You'll learn about printing database records with FileMaker Pro.

PREVIEWING AND PRINTING REPORTS

THE ABILITY TO create printed reports from a database file is something every database user needs sooner or later. In many cases, a printed report is the final result of your work with a database. You enter and edit records, use the Find command to find just the records you want to show, use the Sort command to put those records in a specific order, and then use the Print command to print the records in one of the layouts you created for the database. These are the natural steps you might follow to convert raw data into a format you can use.

FileMaker Pro lets you print single records, records being browsed, blank layouts, and even field definitions. You can save paper by checking reports in Preview mode before printing them out. In this chapter, you'll learn how to preview and print information in various formats.

SETTING UP FOR PRINTING

Before you print records, you can specify information about the paper you're using and the printer effects you want to use. Select the Page Setup command from the File menu to access the Page Setup dialog box. If you've been using a Macintosh for a while, you've probably encountered the Page Setup dialog box before. Its options are relatively standard among Macintosh applications.

TIP

If you'll be printing your layout with special page settings (not letter-size paper with portrait orientation), it's a good idea to adjust the settings in the Page Setup dialog box before modifying or creating the layout you'll use for the printed version (see Chapters 4 and 5 for details on modifying and creating layouts).

The appearance of the Page Setup dialog box varies depending on the printer you have selected with Apple's Chooser, but each version of the dialog box has many elements in common with the others.

FOR MORE INFORMATION...

*For details on selecting a printer with the Apple Chooser, consult
the manuals that came with your Macintosh.*

If you selected an Apple ImageWriter printer with the Apple Chooser, the Page
Setup dialog box looks something like this:

```
┌─────────────────────────────────────────────────────────────────┐
│  ImageWriter                              7.0        (   OK   )    │
│  Paper:  ⦿ US Letter          ○ A4 Letter                         │
│          ○ US Legal           ○ International Fanfold  ( Cancel )  │
│          ○ Computer Paper     ○ Envelope (#10)                    │
│  Orientation    Special Effects:  ☐ Tall Adjusted                 │
│   [▪][▪]                          ☐ 50 % Reduction                │
│                                   ☐ No Gaps Between Pages          │
│                                                                   │
│  Edit Paper Sizes:                                                │
│       Name: [US Letter            ]        ( Save   )             │
│       Width: [8.500]   Height: [11.000]    (Restore )             │
└─────────────────────────────────────────────────────────────────┘
```

If you've selected an Apple LaserWriter printer with the Apple Chooser, the Page
Setup dialog box looks something like this:

```
┌─────────────────────────────────────────────────────────────────┐
│  LaserWriter Page Setup                   7.0        (   OK   )   │
│  Paper: ⦿ US Letter  ○ A4 Letter                                  │
│         ○ US Legal   ○ B5 Letter  ○ [ Tabloid    ▼]  ( Cancel )   │
│  Reduce or [100]%     Printer Effects:              (Options )    │
│  Enlarge:             ☒ Font Substitution?                        │
│  Orientation          ☒ Text Smoothing?                           │
│   [▪][▪]              ☒ Graphics Smoothing?                       │
│                       ☒ Faster Bitmap Printing?                   │
└─────────────────────────────────────────────────────────────────┘
```

If you've selected a Personal LaserWriter SC printer with the Apple Chooser, the Page Setup dialog box looks something like this:

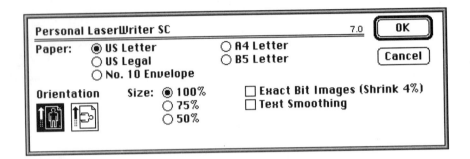

If you've selected a StyleWriter printer with the Apple Chooser, the Page Setup dialog box looks something like this:

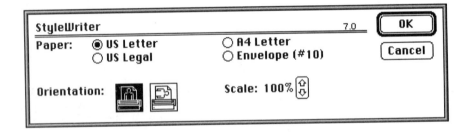

Let's review some of the common options available for these four printers. If your printer is not one of these types, you'll probably find that it offers some or all of the same options.

FOR MORE INFORMATION...

For details on all the paper-size options and the printer effects your printer supports, consult the manual that came with your printer.

- **Paper Size:** You can select a paper size from among several standards. Most often, you'll use US Letter, which is $8\frac{1}{2} \times 11$ inch paper. Other times, you might use US Legal, which is $8\frac{1}{2} \times 14$ inch paper. The ImageWriter Page Setup dialog box allows you to specify a custom paper size, which you can then save for future use. The LaserWriter offers a pop-up menu of additional paper sizes. To select a paper size, click on the radio button beside the paper size you want to use.

- **Orientation:** Choose one of the two orientations: portrait (upright) or landscape (sideways). Portrait orientation is the most common, but you can switch to landscape by clicking on the icon for that orientation.

- **Special or Printer Effects:** For printers that support special or printer effects, you will see check boxes that let you turn the effects on or off. Normally, you won't change any of these settings once they're set up the way you want them. In fact, the default settings are usually fine for most purposes.

- **Reduce or Enlarge:** Most printers offer at least one size option. Specify a percentage to reduce or enlarge by entering it in an edit box, clicking on a check box or radio button, or using arrow icons to increase or reduce the percentage.

In addition to these options, clicking on the Options button in the Page Setup dialog box for the LaserWriter displays the LaserWriter Options dialog box.

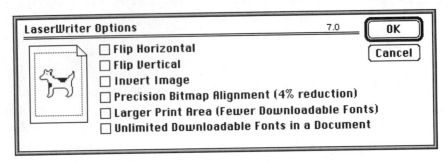

In this dialog box, you can set other options to specify how the printout should appear.

PREVIEWING YOUR REPORTS

Preview mode gives you a good idea of what your document will look like when it is printed. You can switch to Preview mode by choosing the Preview command from the Select menu or by selecting Preview from the Mode pop-up menu at the bottom of the FileMaker Pro window.

SHORTCUT
You can use the ⌘-U key combination to switch to Preview mode.

When you switch to Preview mode, the FileMaker Pro window displays the records in the current layout. If the current layout is a columnar report, the window may look something like this:

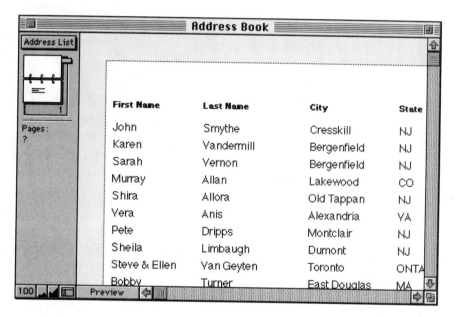

In this mode, the book lets you scroll through pages. The Pages indicator beneath the book shows a question mark (?) because FileMaker Pro does not know how many pages there are until it displays the last page of the report. If you click on the bottom page of the book until you get to the last page, the final page number appears here.

You can view a reduced version of the page by clicking on the zoom control button at the bottom of the window.

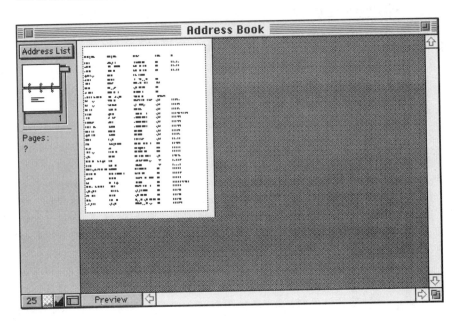

TIP

Use both Preview and Layout modes to fine-tune your reports before committing them to paper.

PRINTING A HARD COPY

SHORTCUT

In any mode, the ⌘–P key combination accesses the Print dialog box.

When you want to print a hard copy that you can share with others and keep for your own records, use the Print command on the File menu. You see the Print dialog box, in which you specify how and what to print. Like the Page Setup dialog box, the Print dialog box varies depending on the printer you specified with Apple's Chooser.

If you selected an Apple ImageWriter printer with the Apple Chooser, the Print dialog box looks something like this:

```
 ImageWriter                                    7.0       ┌─────────┐
                                                          │  Print  │
 Quality:      ○ Best      ◉ Faster   ○ Draft             └─────────┘
 Page Range:   ◉ All       ○ From: [    ] To: [    ]       ┌─────────┐
 Copies:       [ 1 ]                                       │ Cancel  │
                                                          └─────────┘
 Paper Feed:   ◉ Automatic    ○ Hand Feed

 Number pages from: [ 1 ]               ☐ Color ribbon installed

 Print:  ◉ Records being browsed        ☐ Enable Print Spooling
         ○ Current record
         ○ Blank record, showing fields  [ as formatted ]
         ○ Script:  [ All scripts        ]
         ○ Field definitions
```

If you selected an Apple LaserWriter printer with the Apple Chooser, the Print dialog box looks something like this:

```
LaserWriter  "LaserWriter"                          7.0    [ Print ]

Copies: [1]        Pages: ◉ All  ○ From: [   ]  To: [   ]    [ Cancel ]

Cover Page:    ◉ No ○ First Page  ○ Last Page
Paper Source: ◉ Paper Cassette   ○ Manual Feed
Print:           ◉ Black & White   ○ Color/Grayscale
Destination:   ◉ Printer          ○ PostScript® File

Number pages from: [1]

Print:  ◉ Records being browsed
        ○ Current record
        ○ Blank record, showing fields [ as formatted ]
        ○ Script: [ All scripts ]
        ○ Field definitions
```

If you selected an Apple Personal LaserWriter SC printer with the Apple Chooser, the Print dialog box looks something like this:

```
Personal LaserWriter SC                             7.0    [ Print ]

Copies: [1]     Pages: ◉ All  ○ From: [   ]  To: [   ]      [ Cancel ]

Paper Source: ◉ Paper Cassette   ○ Manual Feed


Number pages from: [1]

Print:  ◉ Records being browsed
        ○ Current record
        ○ Blank record, showing fields [ as formatted ]
        ○ Script: [ All scripts ]
        ○ Field definitions
```

If you selected an Apple StyleWriter printer with the Apple Chooser, the Print
dialog box looks something like this:

```
┌─────────────────────────────────────────────────────────────┐
│ StyleWriter                              7.0    [  Print  ]   │
│                                                                │
│ Copies:   [ 1 ]      Quality:   ◉ Best   ○ Faster  [ Cancel ] │
│                                                                │
│ Pages:   ◉ All   ○ From: [    ]  To: [    ]                    │
│                                                                │
│ Paper:   ◉ Sheet Feeder   ○ Manual                            │
│                                                                │
│ Number pages from:  [ 1 ]                                     │
│                                                                │
│ Print:  ◉ Records being browsed                               │
│         ○ Current record                                      │
│         ○ Blank record, showing fields [ as formatted  ]      │
│         ○ Script: [ All scripts            ]                  │
│         ○ Field definitions                                   │
└─────────────────────────────────────────────────────────────┘
```

The Print dialog box options can be divided into two categories: standard printing
options and FileMaker Pro printing options.

STANDARD PRINTING OPTIONS

The options for the different types of printers are similar. If you've been working
with a Macintosh for a while, many of the settings will be familiar to you.

FOR MORE INFORMATION...
*For details on all the print options your printer supports, consult
the manual that came with your printer.*

Here are some of the most common standard printing options:

▸ **Copies:** This edit box lets you enter the number of copies of each page you
want printed. You can enter any whole number from 1 to 99. The default
value is 1.

**PREVIEWING
AND PRINTING REPORTS**
. . . .

CH. 9

▸ **Pages (Page Range):** The Print dialog box gives you the option of printing all or a range of pages. Use the radio buttons to select All or From/To. If you select From/To, enter the starting and ending page numbers for the page range. The default setting is All pages.

▸ **Paper Source (Paper Feed):** These radio buttons let you tell your printer how you will feed it paper. Although the terminology varies from printer to printer, you're offered a choice between automatic (or cassette fed) paper and manually fed paper. Whatever method you used the last time you printed (even if it was in another application) is the method that is selected when you open the Print dialog box.

▸ **Other Options:** Depending on your printer, the Print dialog box may contain options for quality, cover page, colors, destination, and print spooling.

FILEMAKER PRO PRINTING OPTIONS

The options in the lower half of the Print dialog box are specific to FileMaker Pro. You won't find these options in the Print dialog box of other applications. The program-specific printing options are the same for all printers.

▸ **Number Pages From:** This edit box lets you enter the starting page number to be printed on your FileMaker Pro report. If you have not instructed FileMaker Pro to print the page number on your report (with the ## key combination, as explained in Chapter 5), you don't need to use this option. Don't confuse the Number Pages From edit box with the Page Range edit boxes near the top of the Print dialog box. The Number Pages From value tells FileMaker Pro what number to start with when printing the page numbers on your report. The Page Range values tell FileMaker Pro which pages to print.

▸ **Print:** These radio buttons offer five printing options: records being browsed, current record, blank record, scripts, and field definitions. The

Print radio button you select determines what FileMaker Pro will print, as described in the following sections.

NEW IN 2.0

FileMaker Pro can now print scripts, which automate repetitious tasks. Scripts are covered in Chapter 12.

PRINTING THE RECORDS BEING BROWSED

Most often, you'll want to print the records *being browsed*; that is, either all the records or the records in the found set.

If necessary, set up the records for printing:

▶ Use the Find command to select records to print (see Chapter 7).

▶ Use the Sort command to put the found set into the order you want to use for printing (see Chapter 8).

▶ Use the Layout pop-up menu above the book to change to the layout you want to use for printing (see Chapters 4 and 5).

Then choose the Print command from the File menu or press ⌘-P to access the Print dialog box. If necessary, indicate the number of copies you need and specify other printing options. Make sure the Records Being Browsed radio button is clicked on, and then click on the Print button. FileMaker Pro prints your report in the current layout.

PRINTING THE CURRENT RECORD

At times, you may only want to print one record. This is most common when you have records on a single page form layout. The current record of a columnar report (or any layout that displays more than one record at a time) is indicated by a dark bar along the left side of the record. In this example, the record for Lynn Brown is the current record:

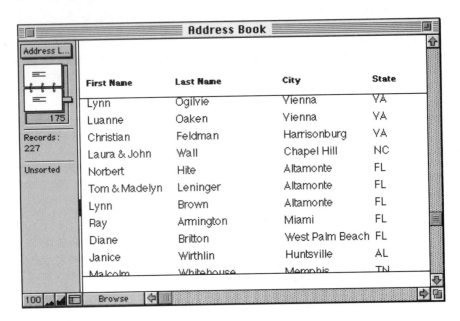

In Browse mode, use the book to find the record you want to print. If necessary, make it the current record by clicking on it. If you want to use another layout for printing, use the Layout pop-up menu to switch to that layout.

Display the Print dialog box. Change the number of copies and other printing settings as necessary. Make sure the Current Record radio button is clicked on, and then click on the Print button. FileMaker Pro prints that one record in the current layout.

PRINTING BLANK LAYOUTS

At times, you might want to print a layout with no records in it at all. This is especially useful if you created a data-entry form to be filled in manually and entered into FileMaker Pro later. It's also useful when you're fine-tuning a layout and can't see it all on your screen.

Switch to the layout you want to use for the printout and display the Print dialog box. If necessary, indicate the number of copies you need and specify other printer options. Make sure the Blank Record radio button is clicked on.

When the Blank Record button is selected, you can pull down the pop-up menu at the end of the option to see the field-formatting options.

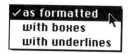

These options determine how the fields will appear on the blank form:

▸ **As Formatted:** With this option selected, the fields will print exactly the way they are formatted in Layout mode. For example, if the fields are formatted to display boxes around them, that's the way they will print. If they're formatted without boxes or any special formatting, only empty spaces will be printed.

▸ **With Boxes:** With this option selected, the fields will print with boxes around them, regardless of how they are formatted in Layout mode.

▸ **With Underlines:** With this option selected, the fields will print with baselines only, regardless of how they are formatted in Layout mode.

After you select a field format, click on the Print button. FileMaker Pro prints a single blank record in the current layout.

PRINTING FIELD DEFINITIONS

When you choose to print field definitions, FileMaker Pro generates a list of all the fields you defined for your database. This is a useful document if you have many fields and have trouble keeping track of them. The list includes the field name, field type, calculation and summary field formulas, and any entry options. FileMaker Pro also places a header and footer on the printout.

Access the Print dialog box, indicate the number of copies you need, and specify other printer options as necessary. Make sure the Field Definitions radio button is clicked on, and then click on the Print button. FileMaker Pro prints the field definitions for all the fields in your database.

IN THIS CHAPTER, you learned how to use the Page Setup dialog box, Preview mode, and the Print dialog box. Through the Print dialog box, you can print five different types of reports. You can use the Find, Sort, and Print commands in conjunction with records and layouts to produce reports that include only the information you want to show, just the way you want to show it.

In the next chapter, you'll start working with one of FileMaker Pro's more advanced features: the ability to summarize information. You'll learn about summary fields and parts and how to use them to create totals and subtotals for your reports.

SUMMARIZING INFORMATION

BY USING SUMMARY fields and summary parts, you can summarize information in your database. Columnar reports, especially those containing financial or numerical data, can be greatly enhanced with the inclusion of grand totals and subtotals.

In this chapter, you'll learn how to include totals and subtotals for specified fields. You can see the totals while you're in Browse mode, as well as in the printout. Subtotals appear only in Preview mode and on printed pages.

WORKING WITH SUMMARY FIELDS AND PARTS

A *summary field* is one of the seven field types you can define for a FileMaker Pro database. As when you create a calculation field, you enter a formula for a new summary field. But while a calculation field contains the result of a formula for *one record*, a summary field contains the result of a formula calculated for *a group of records*. Your summary fields can contain formulas for totals, subtotals, averages, counts, and a number of other summary calculations.

In order to use a summary field, you must place it in a *summary part*. The three types of summary parts are *leading grand summary*, *trailing grand summary*, and *sub-summary*.

The two kinds of grand summary parts summarize information for the found set.

The summary fields in a grand summary part summarize all the records being browsed. When you use the Find command to select some of the records in the database, the values in the summary fields will change.

Ace Computer Supply
Inventory Report

As of 10/5/93

Part Name	Number	Stock Date	Unit Price	On Hand	Total Value
SS Software	D-6748	01/25/93	$91.04	67	$6,099.68
SS Software	D-9565	02/22/93	$56.60	55	$3,113.00
WP Software	D-0718	04/15/93	$90.83	57	$5,177.31
Utility Software	D-1919	01/25/93	$73.10	16	$1,169.60
Graphics Software	D-3296	02/03/93	$38.40	79	$3,033.60
Graphics Software	D-4142	06/25/93	$30.58	33	$1,009.14
Utility Software	D-3762	12/18/92	$71.31	52	$3,708.12
WP Software	D-0622	06/28/93	$43.37	84	$3,643.08
SS Software	D-9392	05/08/93	$89.90	25	$2,247.50
WP Software	D-4209	01/09/93	$4.84	88	$425.92
SS Software	D-3080	04/17/93	$45.15	94	$4,244.10
Grand Total				650	$33,871.05

A sub-summary part summarizes information for a group of records that share the same value in one field.

Ace Computer Supply   As of 10/5/93
Inventory Report

Part Name	Number	Stock Date	Unit Price	On Hand	Total Value
Graphics Software	D-3296	02/03/93	$38.40	79	$3,033.60
Graphics Software	D-4142	06/25/93	$30.58	33	$1,009.14
Graphics Software Total				112	$4,042.74
SS Software	D-6748	01/25/93	$91.04	67	$6,099.68
SS Software	D-9565	02/22/93	$56.60	55	$3,113.00
SS Software	D-9392	05/08/93	$89.90	25	$2,247.50
SS Software	D-3080	04/17/93	$45.15	94	$4,244.10
SS Software Total				241	$15,704.28
Utility Software	D-1919	01/25/93	$73.10	16	$1,169.60
Utility Software	D-3762	12/18/92	$71.31	52	$3,708.12
Utility Software Total				68	$4,877.72
WP Software	D-0718	04/15/93	$90.83	57	$5,177.31
WP Software	D-0622	06/28/93	$43.37	84	$3,643.08
WP Software	D-4209	01/09/93	$4.84	88	$425.92
WP Software Total				229	$9,246.31
Grand Total				650	$33,871.05

When you create a sub-summary part, you specify which field you want to summarize by. After you place summary fields into the part, you sort the database or found set by the field you are summarizing by. Sorting groups the records by the value in that field (see Chapter 8).

The summary fields in the sub-summary part summarize the records in each group. In a report, there will be a sub-summary part for each value in the field you summarize by. Sub-summary parts appear in Preview mode or in the printed report.

In this chapter, you'll learn how to use summary fields and parts to add information to your database.

CREATING A SUMMARY FIELD

You begin defining a summary field in the same way that you define other types of
fields (see Chapter 2). Press ⌘–Shift-D or choose Define Fields from the Select
menu to access the Define Fields dialog box. In the Name edit box, enter the name
of the field you want to create. Then click on the radio button beside Summary in
the Type area.

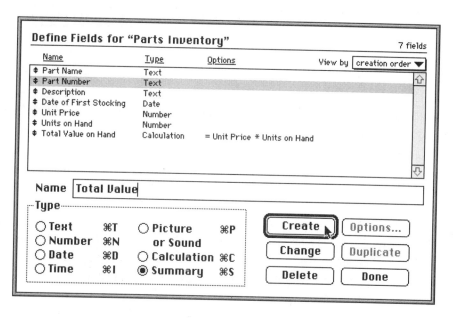

When you click on the Create button, the Summary Field dialog box appears. This
dialog box lets you select a calculation to perform and the field on which to perform it.

SELECTING A SUMMARY FIELD FORMULA

The pop-up menu on the left side of the Summary Field dialog box lists the predefined formulas.

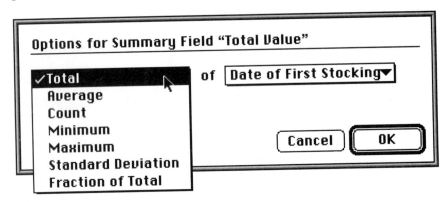

Choose the formula you want to use in the summary field. The calculations performed by these formulas are described in the following sections.

TOTAL

The Total formula adds all the values of a field. It lets you create grand totals (in a grand summary part) or subtotals (in a sub-summary part). When you select Total, a check box for Running Total appears beneath the pop-up menu.

Choose the formula you want to use in the summary field. The calculations performed by these formulas are described in the following sections.

When the Running Total check box is selected, FileMaker Pro calculates running totals. The running total feature is useful only for summary fields used in sub-summary parts.

AVERAGE

The Average formula calculates the average of all the values in a field. When you select Average, a check box for Weighted By appears beneath the pop-up menu. When this is also selected, FileMaker Pro offers another pop-up menu so that you can select a field to use for weighting the average.

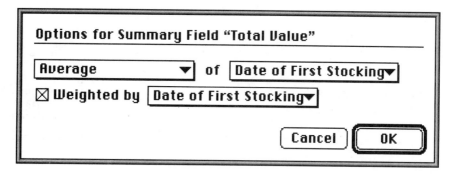

COUNT

The Count formula counts all the records that contain a value in a field. When you select Count, a check box for Running Count appears beneath the pop-up menu.

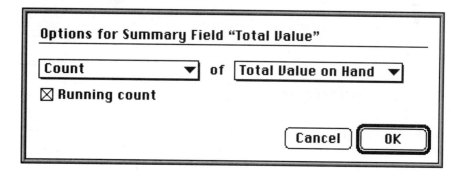

When the Running Count check box is selected, FileMaker Pro calculates running counts. The running count feature is useful only for summary fields used in sub-summary parts.

MINIMUM, MAXIMUM, AND STANDARD DEVIATION

The Minimum formula finds the minimum value for a field, and the Maximum formula finds the maximum value for a field. The Standard Deviation formula calculates the standard deviation from the mean (average) of the values in a field.

FRACTION OF TOTAL

The Fraction of Total formula calculates the ratio of the values in a field to the total of all the values in that field for the found set. When you select Fraction of Total, a check box for Subtotaled when Sorted By appears beneath the pop-up menu. When the Subtotaled when Sorted By check box is selected, FileMaker Pro offers another pop-up menu so that you can select a field to sort by when calculating the fraction of total.

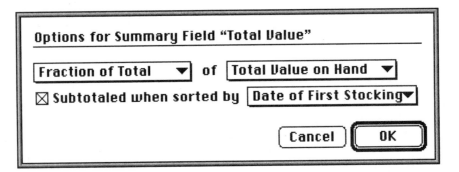

SELECTING THE FIELD TO SUMMARIZE

The pop-up menu on the right side of the Summary Field dialog box lists the fields in the database.

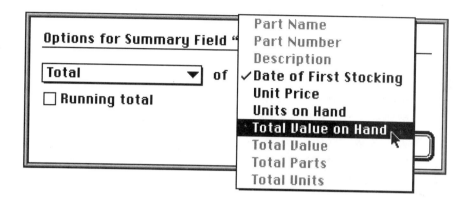

On this pop-up menu, you can select only the fields that the calculation you chose can be applied to. Fields you cannot select appear gray. For example, you cannot total a text field, so all the text fields are shown in gray when you select the Total formula.

Select the field you want to summarize and click on OK. The summary field and its definition appear in the Field List window in the Define Fields dialog box.

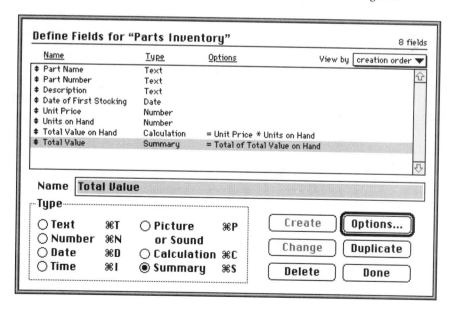

When you're finished defining fields, click on Done. You are returned to whatever mode you were in before you accessed the Define Fields dialog box.

NOTE

If you checked the Add Newly Defined Fields to Current Layout option in the Preferences dialog box (displayed by the Preferences command on the File menu), the field you defined, along with its field label, will appear on the current layout. Setting preferences is discussed in Chapter 12.

SETTING UP A GRAND SUMMARY PART

You can use the summary fields you've defined in a grand summary part to summarize a field. After you create the part and add fields to it, you can view your grand summaries in several ways.

CREATING A GRAND SUMMARY PART

You create a grand summary part in the same way that you create other parts (see Chapter 5). Use the Layout pop-up menu to switch to the layout on which you want the grand summary part to appear. Grand summary parts are most useful in columnar reports, but they can be used in other kinds of layouts as well.

In Layout mode, use the part tool to position the new part. To create a leading grand summary, place the part tool on the body. To create a trailing grand summary, position the part tool below the body.

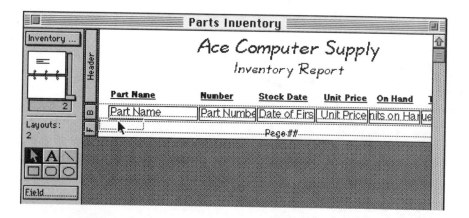

When you release the part tool, the Part Definition dialog box appears. Click on the radio button for Leading Grand Summary or Trailing Grand Summary.

Part Definition

○ Title Header
○ Header
○ Leading Grand Summary
○ Body
○ Sub-Summary when sorted by:
● Trailing Grand Summary
○ Footer
○ Title Footer

Part Name
Part Number
Description
Date of First Stocking
Unit Price
Units on Hand
Total Value on Hand
Total Value

☐ Page break before each occurrence
☐ Page break after every [   ] occurrences
☐ Restart page numbers after each occurrence
☐ Allow part to break across page boundaries
    ☐ Discard remainder of part before new page

[Cancel]
[OK]

SUMMARIZING
INFORMATION
. . . .

CH. 10

Then click on OK. A new part appears on your layout.

NOTE

Only certain types of parts are available in the Part Definition dialog box, depending on where you drag the part tool. If neither of the grand summary parts is a choice, click on Cancel and reposition the part tool until a grand summary part is an option.

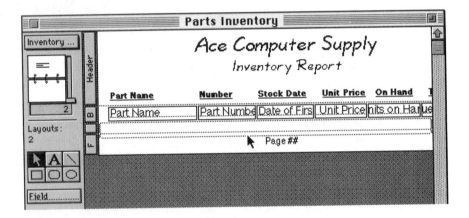

If necessary, resize the grand summary part so that a field can fit into it (resizing parts is described in Chapter 5).

Now you can add summary fields to the grand summary part. Drag the field tool onto the layout to a position in the grand summary part. When you release the tool, the New Field dialog box appears.

TIP

Placing a summary field beneath the field it summarizes in a columnar report helps identify it as a summary of that field. Use the field tool to precisely position the field when you add it to the layout, or move it into position after it has been added (see Chapter 4).

Click on the name of the summary field you want to place in the grand summary part. Use the Create Field Label check box to include or exclude a label for the summary field. Then click on OK to add the field to the grand summary part.

Continue to add the other summary fields you want to include in the grand summary part.

While you're still in Layout mode, you may want to format the summary fields, add text or graphics, or make other layout changes.

VIEWING A GRAND SUMMARY

You can view your grand summary parts in three different ways: in Browse mode, in Preview mode, and on a printed report.

NOTE
In some of the illustrations in this chapter, the status area was hidden by clicking on the status area control button. Without the status area, you can see more of your layout, which is especially useful on small-screen Macintosh models.

A GRAND SUMMARY IN BROWSE MODE

You can see a grand summary part in Browse mode. If you want to view a trailing grand summary part, use the vertical scroll bar to scroll to the last record being browsed. Right below it, you'll find the part and the fields it contains.

Parts Inventory

Ace Computer Supply
Inventory Report
As of 10/5/93
Page ?

Part Name	Number	Stock Date	Unit Price	On Hand	Total Value
Phone Net	C-3336	07/07/93	$46.56	12	$558.72
Math	A-8142	07/04/93	$29.87	18	$537.66
Disk Case	B-9609	12/26/92	$6.20	66	$409.20
Disk Box	B-7026	06/18/93	$42.45	75	$3,183.75
WP Software	D-4209	01/09/93	$4.84	88	$425.92
Calendar	B-3298	01/06/93	$12.94	64	$828.16
SS Software	D-3080	04/17/93	$45.15	94	$4,244.10
				Grand Total	$160,463.10

100	Browse

To view a leading grand summary, scroll to the first record. The leading grand summary part appears above it.

You can experiment with the database and grand summary part while in Browse mode. Try changing one of the values that is summarized. Or use the Find command to narrow down the selection of records. When you change the data or the records being browsed, the summary values also change.

A GRAND SUMMARY IN PREVIEW MODE

When you switch to Preview mode, your grand summary part appears how it will look when printed. A leading grand summary should appear above the first record on the first page of the report.

To view a trailing grand summary, use the book to move to the last page. This may take a while if your layout is complex, the found set is large, or your computer is slow. The trailing grand summary part appears after the last record on the last page.

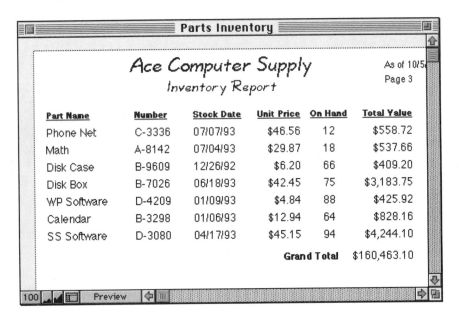

SETTING UP A SUB-SUMMARY PART

Sub-summary parts are a bit trickier than grand summary parts. They let you create subtotals, but they depend upon the database being properly sorted to work. For example, you could create a sub-summary part that summarizes information when the database is sorted by the Product Name field of a parts inventory database.

CREATING A SUB-SUMMARY PART

Use the Layout pop-up menu to switch to the layout you want to contain the sub-summary part. Like grand summary parts, sub-summary parts are most useful in columnar reports, but they can be used in other layouts.

In Layout mode, drag the part tool onto the layout to a position on or below the body.

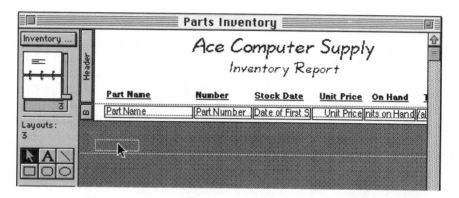

Release the part tool. In the Part Definition dialog box, click on the radio button for Sub-Summary and click on OK. The Sort By scrolling window becomes active.

Click on the name of the field you want to use to group your sub-summary.

The field you choose should contain values that are common to more than one record. For example, you would not select a serial number field, because serial numbers are normally unique from record to record. FileMaker Pro will create as many subtotals as it needs to represent each group of information.

Click on OK. A new part appears on your layout. If necessary, resize the part so that a field can fit into it.

Use the field tool to add fields to the sub-summary part. After you finish adding fields, you can modify the layout while you're still in Layout mode.

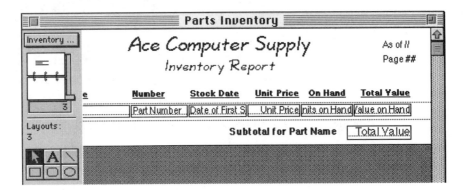

WARNING

You must *sort the database or found set by the field you specified in the Part Definition dialog box. If you do not sort the data, FileMaker Pro cannot prepare sub-summaries. Sorting records is described in Chapter 8.*

After you've set up your sub-summary part, access the Sort dialog box by selecting Sort from the Select menu or by using the ⌘-S shortcut. Create a sort order that sorts by the field you specified in the Part Definition dialog box for the sub-summary part.

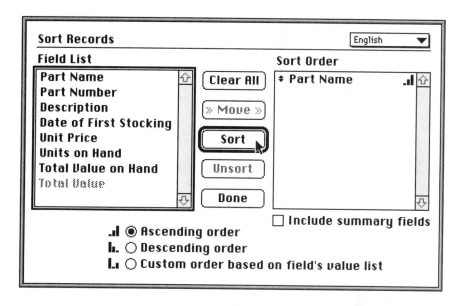

Click on Sort. FileMaker Pro sorts the information, and your sub-summary is ready for viewing.

VIEWING A SUB-SUMMARY

 NOTE

You cannot see sub-summaries in Browse mode.

You can view your sub-summary part in Preview mode or on a printed report. When you scroll through pages in Preview mode, you'll notice how the records are grouped by the values in the field you sorted by. You'll also see the sub-summaries before or after the group of records.

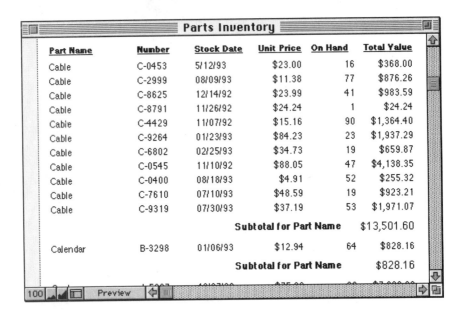

Part Name	Number	Stock Date	Unit Price	On Hand	Total Value
Cable	C-0453	5/12/93	$23.00	16	$368.00
Cable	C-2999	08/09/93	$11.38	77	$876.26
Cable	C-8625	12/14/92	$23.99	41	$983.59
Cable	C-8791	11/26/92	$24.24	1	$24.24
Cable	C-4429	11/07/92	$15.16	90	$1,364.40
Cable	C-9264	01/23/93	$84.23	23	$1,937.29
Cable	C-6802	02/25/93	$34.73	19	$659.87
Cable	C-0545	11/10/92	$88.05	47	$4,138.35
Cable	C-0400	08/18/93	$4.91	52	$255.32
Cable	C-7610	07/10/93	$48.59	19	$923.21
Cable	C-9319	07/30/93	$37.19	53	$1,971.07
			Subtotal for Part Name		$13,501.60
Calendar	B-3298	01/06/93	$12.94	64	$828.16
			Subtotal for Part Name		$828.16

When you view the records in Browse mode, you'll see that the sort order is maintained, but the sub-summaries disappear. Unsort the records or sort by a different field and then try Preview mode again. You'll find that the sub-summaries are gone.

When you are working with sub-summary parts, keep in mind two important rules: the database must be correctly sorted and you must view the results in Preview mode or a printout.

COMBINING SUMMARY TYPES

You can create a report with sub-summaries and a grand summary by creating a layout with both a grand summary part and a sub-summary part.

Here's an example of a layout with both trailing grand summary and sub-summary parts.

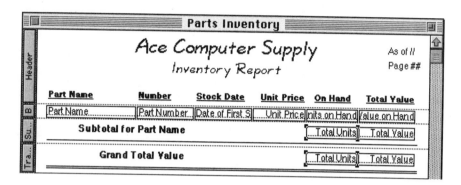

Notice how the same two summary fields are included in both parts. The layout also includes some lines (added with the line tool in Layout mode). The lines work with the parts to separate the groups. In Preview mode, the last records on the last page of the layout appear like this:

Subtotal for Part Name				145	$3,762.32
UPS	F-0406	10/05/93	$93.34	40	$3,733.60
Subtotal for Part Name				40	$3,733.60
Utility Software	D-5726	07/08/93	$64.98	90	$5,848.20
Utility Software	D-1919	01/25/93	$73.10	16	$1,169.60
Utility Software	D-3762	12/18/92	$71.31	52	$3,708.12
Subtotal for Part Name				158	$10,725.92
WP Software	D-8624	08/26/93	$39.14	29	$1,135.06
WP Software	D-0718	04/15/93	$90.83	57	$5,177.31
WP Software	D-0622	06/28/93	$43.37	84	$3,643.08
WP Software	D-4209	01/09/93	$4.84	88	$425.92
Subtotal for Part Name				258	$10,381.37
Grand Total Value				4,077	$174,030.29

USING MULTIPLE SUB-SUMMARY PARTS

Once you've mastered working with one sub-summary, you're ready to tackle working with two or more. Using multiple sub-summaries might be useful when your records contain data that can be sorted and categorized by more than one field at a time.

For example, here's a database used to keep track of hours worked by different employees of a small restaurant. As you can see, there are many repeated values.

Thursday's Restaurant
Time Report

Date	Name	Hours	Position	Pay
10/5/93	Tom	4.75	Server	$23.75
10/5/93	Madelyn	8.00	Server	$50.00
10/5/93	Laura	8.00	Server	$48.00
10/5/93	Norbert	10.00	Chef	$150.00
10/5/93	Mary	7.00	Hostess	$31.50
10/5/93	Michael	7.50	Kitchen	$37.50
10/5/93	Julie	4.00	Kitchen	$22.00
10/5/93	Frank	5.75	Bus	$25.88
10/5/93	Tammy	7.00	Server	$45.50
10/5/93	John	4.00	Bus	$19.00
10/6/93	Tom	4.00	Server	$20.00
10/6/93	Madelyn	8.00	Server	$50.00
10/6/93	Norbert	10.00	Chef	$150.00
10/6/93	Mary	8.50	Hostess	$38.25
10/6/93	Julie	8.00	Kitchen	$44.00
10/6/93	Frank	9.00	Bus	$40.50
10/6/93	Bill	6.00	Server	$39.00

Suppose that you want subtotals for the Hours Worked and Pay fields by day and within each day, subtotaled by position. This will give you a better idea of how your employee expenses are distributed. You also want grand totals for the Hours Worked and Pay fields.

To set up this report, you would create summary fields that total the Hours Worked and Pay fields.

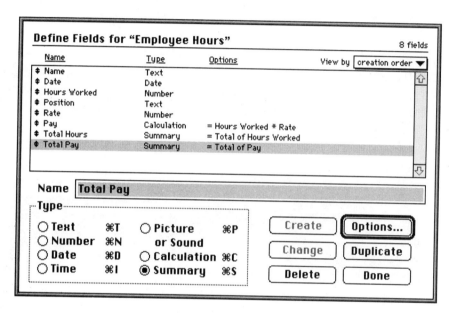

SUMMARIZING
INFORMATION
. . . .

CH. 10

Select a layout for the sub-summary and grand summary parts. In Layout mode, use the part tool to add two sub-summaries beneath the body. The first should be a sub-summary when sorted by Position. The second should be a sub-summary when sorted by Date. Then add a trailing grand summary beneath both sub-summaries.

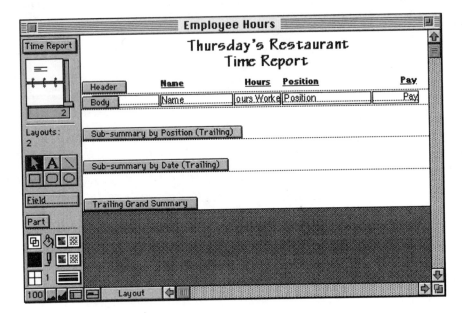

Use the field tool to add the two summary fields to all three new parts.

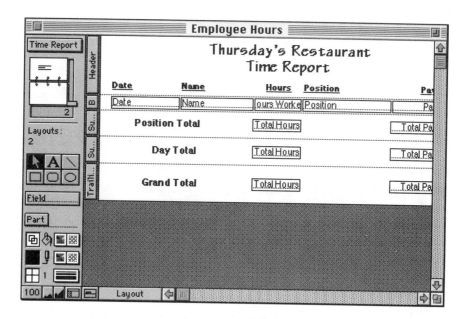

TIP

To save time adding fields, you can add the fields to one part, select them both, use the Copy command to copy them to the clipboard, and then paste them into the other two parts.

Next, sort the records by the Date and Position fields. Note that this is in the opposite order that you want to show subtotals.

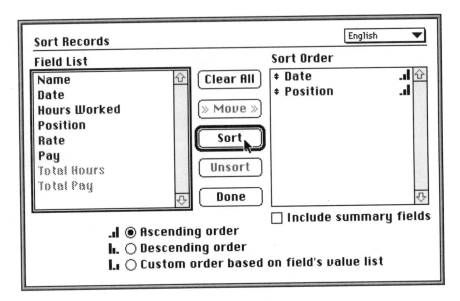

Finally, view the records in Preview mode. Scroll down to see the subtotals and grand total. The following figure shows what the first day might look like when printed.

Thursday's Restaurant
Time Report

Date	Name	Hours	Position	Pay
10/5/93	Frank	5.75	Bus	$25.88
10/5/93	John	4.00	Bus	$19.00
Position Total		9.75		$44.88
10/5/93	Norbert	10.00	Chef	$150.00
Position Total		10.00		$150.00
10/5/93	Mary	7.00	Hostess	$31.50
Position Total		7.00		$31.50
10/5/93	Michael	7.50	Kitchen	$37.50
10/5/93	Julie	4.00	Kitchen	$22.00
Position Total		11.50		$59.50
10/5/93	Tom	4.75	Server	$23.75
10/5/93	Madelyn	8.00	Server	$50.00
10/5/93	Laura	8.00	Server	$48.00
10/5/93	Tammy	7.00	Server	$45.50
Position Total		27.75		$167.25
Day Total		66.00		$453.13

Using multiple sub-summaries in a layout is not difficult. Just be sure to plan your layout beforehand and check your results in Preview mode or a printout before depending on them.

CREATING SUMMARY REPORTS

So far all the examples we've used in this chapter show not only the summaries, but also the detailed data. However, you can summarize data without including the details. This is especially useful if you have a large database and don't want to show every single record in your reports.

Think for a moment about layouts and layout parts. In each layout, the detailed information is included in the same kind of part: the body. By excluding the body from a layout, you exclude the detail. It's as simple as that. Well, not exactly. If you don't plan ahead and include identifying fields in the sub-summary part, you might have a summary and not know what it's for!

Suppose that you want to start with the layout shown in the previous section and modify it to include only the sub-summaries and trailing grand summary. You want to label the sub-summaries with actual field names.

You would use the field tool to add the Position field to the first sub-summary and the Date field to the second sub-summary.

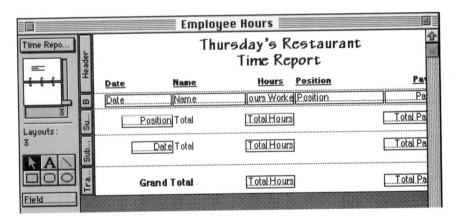

In this example, the word *Total* was added after each field as a text object and put in the same format as the field beside it. When previewed or printed, these paired objects will form identifying phrases for the sub-summary parts.

Delete the body part and any unnecessary field labels in the header. Make any other changes to the layout to close up space and improve the appearance.

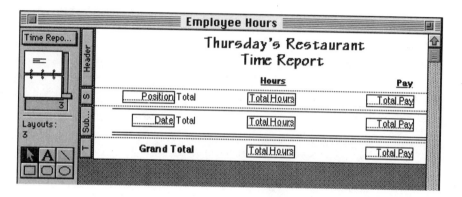

Sort the records by the Date and Position fields. When you view the results in Preview mode or print the report, it will look something like the following figure.

Thursday's Restaurant
Time Report

	Hours	Pay
Bus Total	9.75	$44.88
Chef Total	10.00	$150.00
Hostess Total	7.00	$31.50
Kitchen Total	11.50	$59.50
Server Total	27.75	$167.25
10/5/93 Total	66.00	$453.13
Bus Total	9.00	$40.50
Chef Total	10.00	$150.00
Hostess Total	8.50	$38.25
Kitchen Total	8.00	$44.00
Server Total	18.00	$109.00
10/6/93 Total	53.50	$381.75
Grand Total	119.50	$834.88

MANAGING PAGE BREAKS

Now that you fully understand how parts work, you're ready to deal with the topic of page breaks. The Part Definition dialog box offers up to five page-break options, depending on which part is selected.

```
┌─────────────────────────────────────────────────────────┐
│  Part Definition                                          │
│  ○ Title Header               ┌────────────────────────┐ │
│  ○ Header                     │ Name                 ⬆ │ │
│  ○ Leading Grand Summary      │ Date                   │ │
│  ● Body                       │ Hours Worked           │ │
│  ○ Sub-Summary when sorted by:│ Position               │ │
│  ○ Trailing Grand Summary     │ Rate                   │ │
│  ○ Footer                     │ Pay                    │ │
│  ○ Title Footer               │ Total Hours            │ │
│                               │ Total Pay            ⬇ │ │
│                               └────────────────────────┘ │
│     ☐ Page break before each occurrence                  │
│     ☐ Page break after every [    ] occurrences          │
│     ☐ Restart page numbers after each occurrence         │
│     ☐ Allow part to break across page boundaries  ┌──────┐│
│         ☐ Discard remainder of part before new page│Cancel││
│                                                    └──────┘│
│                                                    ┌──────┐│
│                                                    │  OK  ││
│                                                    └──────┘│
└─────────────────────────────────────────────────────────┘
```

The options set the page breaks as follows:

▸ **Page Break Before Occurrence:** This option, which is available for sub-summary, body, and trailing grand summary parts, instructs FileMaker Pro to start a new page before it prints the part and its contents.

▸ **Page Break After Every *n* Occurrences**: This option, which is available for sub-summary, grand summary, and body parts, instructs FileMaker Pro to start a new page after every certain number of occurrences of that part. You tell FileMaker Pro how many occurrences by entering a value in the edit box.

▸ **Restart Page Numbers After Each Occurrence:** This option, which is available for all parts except a title footer, instructs FileMaker Pro to automatically begin renumbering the pages starting at 1 after it prints that part.

▸ **Allow Part to Break Across Page Boundaries:** This option, which is available for sub-summary, grand summary, and body parts, tells FileMaker Pro that it can put a page break in the middle of that part if the whole part doesn't fit on the page.

▸ **Discard Remainder of Part Before New Page:** This option, which is only available if Allow Part to Break Across Page Boundaries is also selected, instructs FileMaker Pro to print as much of that part as will fit on a page and then forget about printing the rest of the part.

NEW IN 2.0
FileMaker Pro now includes the Discard Remainder of Part Before New Page option.

These options, when used together, provide some control over page breaks in your printed reports. Experiment with them and view the results in Preview mode to insert the page breaks you need.

IN THIS CHAPTER, you learned how to use summary fields and parts to summarize information. You saw that summary parts perform calculations on groups of records, and sub-summary parts summarize groups of information based on the values in a field. You know that you can combine grand summary and sub-summary parts for a variety of summarizations. You also took a look at the page-break options in the Part Definition dialog box.

In the next chapter, we'll switch gears entirely and look at some of the special field options FileMaker Pro offers. These options can make data entry easier, check it for accuracy, or automate it entirely.

Increasing Productivity with Field-Entry Options

11

FEATURING

- Defining entry options for fields
- Automatically entering values
- Checking for acceptable values
- Storing multiple values in a field
- Displaying data-entry lists
- Looking up field entries

THE FORMULAS YOU create for calculation and summary fields in your database are examples of *field-entry options*. For calculation and summary fields, File-Maker Pro automatically creates field-entry options based on the formulas you specify when you define the field. In this chapter, you'll explore the other field-entry options FileMaker Pro offers.

Field-entry options are specified as part of a field's definition. You can include field-entry options when you first create a field or you can add them later. However, it's best to include most entry options right from the start, when you're designing your database.

WORKING WITH FIELD-ENTRY OPTIONS

You specify field-entry options through the Entry Options dialog box, which is accessed through the Define Fields dialog box. Select Define Field from the Select menu or press the ⌘–Shift-D key combination to display the Define Fields dialog box. Then click on the name of an existing text or number field in the Field List window or create a new text or number field.

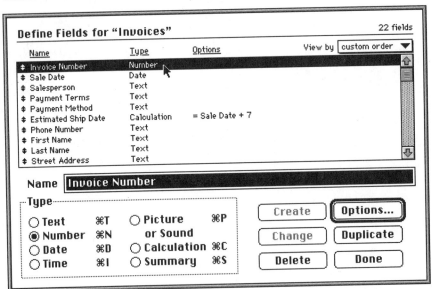

Click on the Options button, and the Entry Options dialog box appears. The Entry Options dialog box can appear two different ways, depending on the type of field you are working with. Text, Number, Date, and Time fields appear like this:

Entry Options for Number Field "Item Number"

Auto-enter a value that is
- ☐ the [Creation Date ▼]
- ☐ a serial number:
- next value [1]
- increment by [1]
- ☐ data [   ]

Verify that the field value is
- ☐ not empty
- ☐ unique ☐ an existing value
- ☐ of type [Number ▼]
- ☐ from [   ]
- to [   ]

☐ Prohibit modification of auto-entered values
☐ Repeating field with a maximum of [2] values
☐ Use a pre-defined value list: [Edit Values...]
☐ Look up values from a file: [Set Lookup...]

[Cancel] [OK]

Calculation fields appear like this:

Options for Field "Extended Price"

Fields:
- Invoice Number
- Sale Date
- Salesperson
- Payment Terms
- Payment Method
- Estimated Ship Date
- Phone Number
- First Name

Operators: = ≠ > < ≥ ≤ and or

Functions:
- Abs (number)
- Atan (number)
- Average (repeating field)
- Cos (number)
- Count (repeating field)
- Date (month, day, year)
- DateToText (date)
- Day (date)

Extended Price =
Unit Price * Units

Calculation result is [Number ▼]
☐ Repeating field with a maximum of [2] values

[Cancel] [OK]

Generally speaking, field-entry options can be separated into three categories: automatic entry options, entry verification options, and customized entry options. The Entry Options dialog box is split into three main parts that correspond to these categories:

- **Auto-entry values:** The auto-entry options instruct FileMaker Pro to automatically enter a value in the field. The value can be a date, time, user name, serial number, or specific piece of information.

- **Verify field values:** The entry verification options check the contents of a field after you enter information into it. You can instruct FileMaker Pro to check to be sure that the field is not empty, contains a unique value, contains an existing value, contains a certain type of value, or fits into a range of values you specify.

- **Customized entry options:** Although not specifically labeled as customized entry options, these four options perform that function. Use these check boxes to tell FileMaker Pro to prohibit modification of any automatically entered values, make the field a repeating field, use a predefined value list, or look up values from another FileMaker Pro file.

USING AUTO-ENTRY VALUES

By having FileMaker Pro automatically enter values into database fields, there's less for you to enter. Not only do these options save data-entry time, but they also ensure that accurate values are entered.

After you select one of these field-entry options, you can see it in action by creating a new record. The new record will automatically contain the data you specified in the appropriate field.

AUTOMATICALLY ENTERING DATES OR TIMES

You may want to automate the entry of dates or times when you need to include the current date or time in a record. For example, in an invoices database, a Sale Date field is a good candidate for an automatically entered date.

To have FileMaker Pro insert the date or time, in the Define Fields dialog box, select the field or create a new field. Then click on Options. In the Entry Options dialog box, click on the first check box under Auto-enter a Value That Is. The pop-up menu beside the word *the* becomes active.

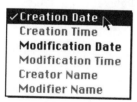

From the pop-up menu, select the auto-enter option you want: creation date, creation time, modification date, modification time, creator name, or modifier name. The type of field determines the auto-enter choices that you can select. In this example, a date field was selected, so only the two date options are available:

NEW IN 2.0

FileMaker Pro can now automatically enter the name of the user who creates or modifies the record. It gets this information from the name of your computer or the custom name information specified in the Preferences dialog box Preferences are discussed in Chapter 12.

Click on OK to accept the change and dismiss the Entry Options dialog box. The Options column of the Field List window now displays a field-entry option for that field.

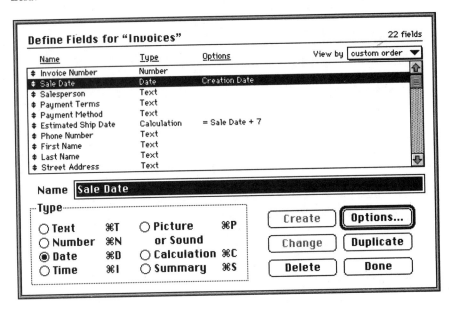

Click on Done in the Define Fields dialog box.

To see how this field-entry option works, create a new record. The new record displays the automatically entered data in the appropriate field. If the field is used in a calculation field (like the field in this example), the calculation field also displays a value.

AUTOMATICALLY ENTERING SERIAL NUMBERS

FileMaker Pro can also assign serial numbers—consecutive numbers often used to identify records—automatically. For example, you might use this option to enter serial numbers in an Invoice Number field.

In the Define Fields dialog box, select the name of the field or create a new field, and then click on Options. In the Entry Options dialog box, click on the second check box under Auto-enter a Value That Is, beside the words *a serial number*. The two edit boxes under this option become active.

```
 Auto-enter a value that is
  [ ] the  [ Creation Date        ▾ ]
  [X] a serial number:
  next value      [ 1                ]
  increment by  [ 1                ]
  [ ] data   [                       ]
```

In the Next Value edit box, enter the starting number for the field. For example, if you want five-digit invoice numbers starting with 00001, enter 00001.

In the Increment By edit box, enter the number you want the serial numbers to increment by. In most cases, this is 1, but if you want to count by 5, 10, 100, or anything else, you can enter that number.

Click on OK to accept the change and dismiss the Entry Options dialog box. The Options column of the Field List window now displays a field-entry option for that field. Click on Done in the Define Fields dialog box.

After you've set up an automatic serial number, the value in the Next Value edit box of the Entry Options dialog box changes according to the increment you specified. If you change this value to a value lower than what is displayed, new records may have the same serial number as existing records.

NEW IN 2.0
You can now automatically re-serialize records by using the Re-place command on the Edit menu.

AUTOMATICALLY ENTERING DATA

Your database may contain a field that always (or almost always) contains the same value. For example, the entry in a Sales Tax Rate field in an invoices data-base might always be the same. Rather than enter that value manually for all records, you can instruct FileMaker Pro to enter it automatically for you.

In the Define Fields dialog box, select the name of the field or create a new field, and then click on Options. In the Entry Options dialog box, click on the third check box under Auto-enter a Value That Is, beside the word *data*. The edit box beside the option becomes active. In the edit box, enter the information you want to appear in every new record you create.

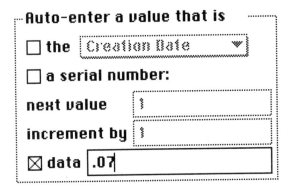

Click on OK in the Entry Options dialog box, and then click on Done in the Define Fields dialog box.

VERIFYING VALUES

The entry verification options check the field to make sure its contents conform with the options you selected. They help ensure that your database contains complete and accurate information. You can use a combination of some of these options to verify entries.

VERIFYING THAT A FIELD IS NOT EMPTY

FileMaker Pro lets you leave fields empty when you enter data in a record. However, when information in a record is important, you may want to be sure you do not neglect to enter it. For example, in an invoices database, you might want to make sure that the customer's phone number is always entered in the Phone Number field. When you tell FileMaker Pro to verify that a field is not empty, it monitors your data-entry activity and checks the field before you move on to another record.

In the Define Fields dialog box, select the name of the field you want to verify isn't blank, or create a new field, and then click on Options. In the Entry Options dialog box, click on the first check box under Verify that the Field Value Is, beside the words *not empty*.

Verify that the field value is
- ☒ not empty
- ☐ unique ☐ an existing value
- ☐ of type [Number ▾]
- ☐ from [   ]
-    to [   ]

Click on OK in the Entry Options dialog box, then on Done in the Define Fields dialog box.

To see this field-entry option in action, create a new record and then try moving to another record without entering data into the field. FileMaker Pro warns you with a dialog box like this:

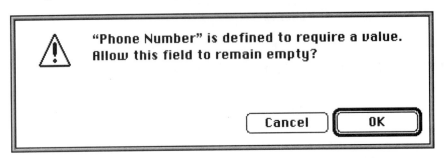

> ⚠ "Phone Number" is defined to require a value. Allow this field to remain empty?
>
> Cancel   OK

Clicking on OK in this dialog box lets you move on to another record without entering data into the field. Clicking on Cancel makes the field the current field so you can enter data before moving on.

VERIFYING THAT A FIELD IS UNIQUE OR AN EXISTING VALUE

If the contents of a field are not the same as the contents of the same field in the rest of the records, the field contents are *unique*. On the other hand, if the contents of the field are the same as the contents of the same field in one or more other records, the field contents are an *existing value*. FileMaker Pro can verify that a field's contents are either unique or an existing value. These two field-entry options are similar in idea but completely opposite in meaning.

A good candidate for a unique value is a serial number, which you wouldn't want repeated in a database. For example, you might require that the Invoice Number field in an invoices database contains unique values.

In the Define Fields dialog box, select the name of the field you want to contain only unique values, or create a new field, and then click on Options. In the Entry

Options dialog box, click on the second check box under Verify that the Field Value Is, beside the word *unique*.

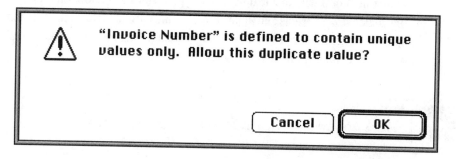

Click on OK in the Entry Options dialog box, and then on Done in the Define Fields dialog box.

To see this field-entry option in action, enter the same value in the field that exists in the same field of another record. A warning dialog box like this should appear:

Clicking on OK in this dialog box tells FileMaker Pro to allow the duplicate value. Clicking on Cancel makes the field the current field so you can edit the value before moving on.

WARNING

If you create a new database and require one of the fields to contain an existing value but do not specify any values, you won't be able to enter data into that field! This option works best in conjunction with predefined value lists, which are covered later in this chapter.

You have FileMaker Pro verify that a field contains an existing value by clicking on the check box next to the words *existing value* under Verify that the Field Value Is in the Entry Options dialog box. When you enter a value that has never been entered in that field before, FileMaker Pro displays a warning dialog box. As with the warnings displayed by field-entry options, you can click on OK to allow the new value or Cancel to edit the value.

VERIFYING THAT A FIELD IS A SPECIFIC TYPE

FileMaker Pro accepts virtually any data in any type of field. You can put text in a number field or a date in a text field. The type verification option in the Entry Options dialog box instructs FileMaker Pro to make sure the data is the type that should be entered. For example, you might want to make sure a Units field always contains a number if that field is used by a calculation field.

NOTE

Fields used in numerical calculations must be numbers to be properly calculated. Text is treated as the number 0 (zero) in numerical calculations.

In the Define Fields dialog box, select the name of the field you want to make sure contains only a certain type of entry, or create a new field, and then click on Options. In the Entry Options dialog box, click on the check box beside the words *of type*, under Verify that the Field Value Is. The pop-up menu beside the option becomes active. From the pop-up menu, select a type: Number, Date, or Time.

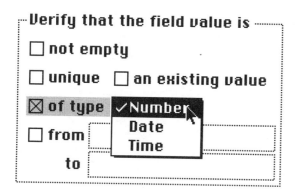

Click on OK in the Entry Options dialog box, then on Done in the Define Fields dialog box.

To try out this field-entry option, enter an inappropriate type value for the field. FileMaker Pro displays a warning dialog box similar to this one:

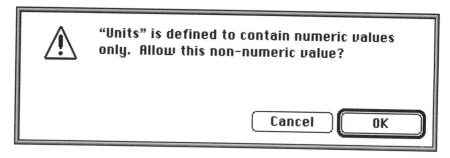

Clicking on OK in this dialog box tells FileMaker Pro to accept the data in the field, even if it isn't the right type. Clicking on Cancel makes the field the current field so you can edit the field's contents before moving on.

VERIFYING THAT A FIELD VALUE IS WITHIN A SPECIFIED RANGE

Another good data test is to verify that a field's value is within an acceptable range. For example, suppose that in your company, sales of more than 100 units should be referred to a manager. You can help prevent salespeople from entering sales for over 100 units by having FileMaker Pro verify that the Units field value is from 0 to 100.

In the Define Fields dialog box, select the name of the field you want to make sure contains values within a specified range, or create a new field, and then click on Options. In the Entry Options dialog box, click on the check box beside the word *from* under Verify that the Field Value Is. The two edit boxes for this option become active. In the From edit box, enter the lower end of the range. In the To edit box, enter the upper end of the range.

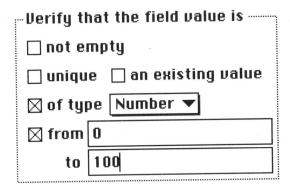

Click on OK in the Entry Options dialog box, then on Done in the Define Fields dialog box.

To see this field-entry option in action, enter a value outside the range you specified for the field. FileMaker Pro displays a warning dialog box similar to this:

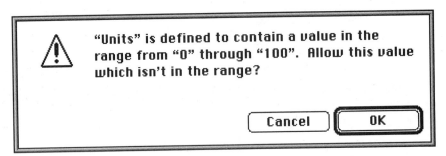

Clicking on OK in this dialog box tells FileMaker Pro to accept the data in the field, even if it isn't within the range. Clicking on Cancel makes the field the current field so you can edit its contents.

PREVENTING CHANGES TO AUTOMATIC ENTRIES

Like any other entry, the values entered automatically by FileMaker Pro can be changed. However, you can make it impossible to edit automatic entries by using the Prohibit Modification of Auto-entered Values option in the Entry Options dialog box. For example, you might want to make sure that a creation date automatically entered in a Sales Date field cannot be changed.

In the Define Fields dialog box, click on the name of a field that has an automatic entry, or create a new field, and then click on Options. In the Entry Options dialog box, click on the check box for Prohibit Modification of Auto-entered Values (near the bottom of the dialog box).

Click on OK in the Entry Options dialog box, then on Done in the Define Fields dialog box.

To see how this field-entry option works, create a new record and then try to change the automatically entered value in the field for which you prohibited modifications. A dialog box appears, telling you that you can't modify the field.

Your only option is to click on OK to dismiss it.

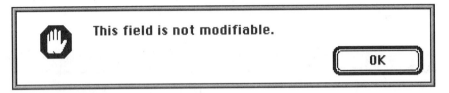

USING REPEATING FIELDS

FileMaker Pro's repeating fields feature makes it possible for a field to contain multiple values. This is useful when you need to store more than one piece of information in a field.

For example, suppose that your invoices database includes an Invoice layout that lets salespeople enter information on an invoice form.

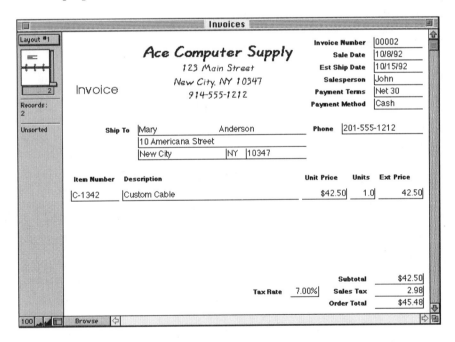

After the sale is entered, not only is the information recorded in the database, but the form can be printed and given or sent to customers. But this database and layout have one drawback: each invoice can be used to sell only one product. If a customer wants to buy several items, several invoices must be prepared. This adds work for the salesperson and prevents management from having an accurate record of the total of each sale.

You can make the Invoice layout work for sales of several items by using repeating fields. With this field-entry option, you can have the Item Number, Description, Unit Price, Units, and Extended Price fields store multiple values. You can even perform calculations on repeating fields by turning a Subtotal field into a calculation field that sums the values in the Extended Price field.

Creating and using repeating fields is a two-step process. The first step is to include the field-entry option for repeating fields in the field's definition. The second step is to format the layout to display the repeating fields.

CREATING REPEATING FIELDS

To create a repeating field, access the Define Fields dialog box and click on the name of a field that you want to turn into a repeating field, or create a new field. Click on Options to display the Entry Options dialog box.

Click on the check box beside the words *Repeating field with a maximum of values* (near the bottom of the dialog box). The Repeating Fields edit box becomes active, with the number 2 in it. In the Repeating Fields edit box, enter the maximum number of values you plan to store in that field. The maximum number is 1,000, but you should use a number that reflects what you expect to need.

☐ Prohibit modification of auto-entered values

☒ Repeating field with a maximum of `10` values

☐ Use a pre-defined value list: [Edit Values...]

☐ Look up values from a file: [Set Lookup...]

Click on OK to accept the change and dismiss the Entry Options dialog box. The repeating field-entry option appears in the Options column of the Field List window for that field, unless it is a calculation field.

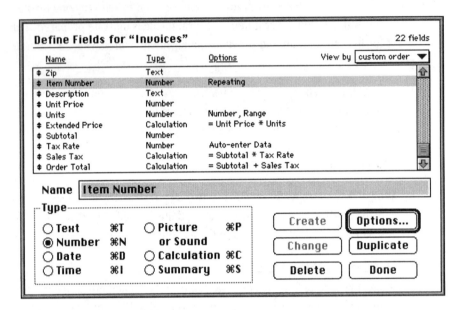

Click on Done in the Define Fields dialog box. Back in Browse or Layout mode, the field should look no different than any other field. Remember, this is a two-step process. The next step is to format the field.

FORMATTING REPEATING FIELDS

The second step to using repeating fields is to instruct FileMaker Pro to show more than one value on the layout. If the field appears on more than one layout, you'll need to format the field on each layout you want to display more than one value.

Switch to Layout mode and click once on the field you want to display as a repeating field to select it. Then select Field Format from the Format menu. The Field Format dialog box appears.

TIP

To change the field layout for more than one repeating field, select all of them at once by holding down the Shift key and clicking on each one.

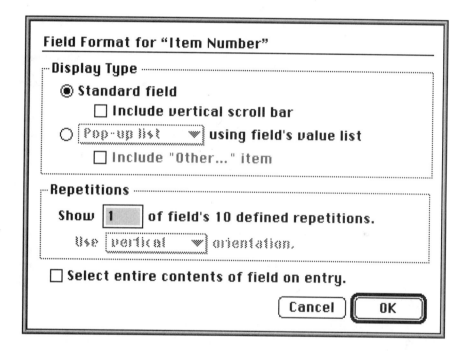

In the Repetitions edit box, enter the number of values you want to appear for the repeating field. The number does not have to be the same as the one you provided in the Entry Options dialog box, but it cannot be higher than that number. When you enter a number (other than 1), the Orientation pop-up menu becomes active.

Use this menu to select from Vertical or Horizontal orientation.

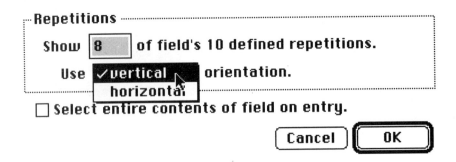

Note that if the field you selected was not defined as a repeating field, you would not be able to enter a value other than 1 in the Repetitions edit box.

Click on OK in the Field Format dialog box. On your layout, the field you formatted now shows spaces for the number of values you specified.

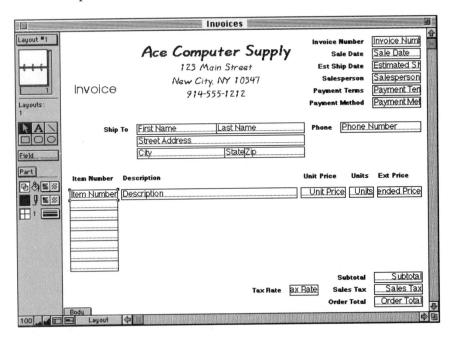

Back in Browse mode, each repeating field you defined and formatted can hold multiple values. Here's the Invoice layout shown at the beginning of this section with the sale of four separate items recorded on it.

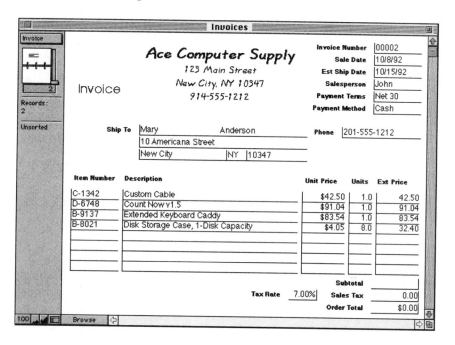

TIP

To include lines around your fields as illustrated here, use the Field Borders command on the Format menu while in Layout mode.

CALCULATING REPEATING FIELDS

In the example above, the Subtotal field is blank. The way that number field is defined, the salesperson must manually add up the extended prices and enter the total in the Subtotal field. You can change the definition of this field so that it sums the contents of the Extended Price field. You need to change that field to a calculation field whose formula contains one of FileMaker Pro's predefined functions.

To change the definition of a field, access the Define Fields dialog box and click on the name of the field you want to change. Click on the Calculation type radio button, then on Change. FileMaker Pro warns you that the data in the field you are changing will be replaced:

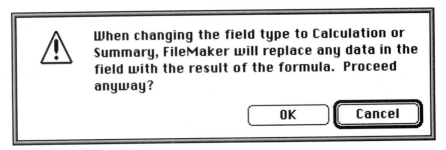

When changing the field type to Calculation or Summary, FileMaker will replace any data in the field with the result of the formula. Proceed anyway?

OK   Cancel

Click on OK to convert the field. The Calculation Field dialog box appears. In the Functions window, double-click on the name of the function you want to use to place it in the Formula edit box. For example, to total the contents of a repeating field, use the Sum (repeating field) function.

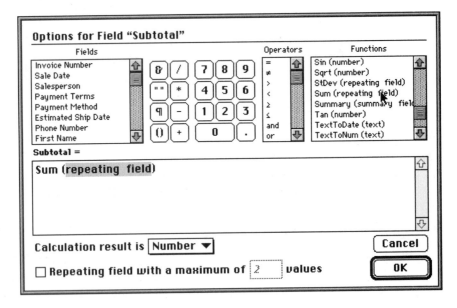

In the Fields window, double-click on the name of the repeating field you want to calculate. FileMaker Pro places it within the parentheses in the formula.

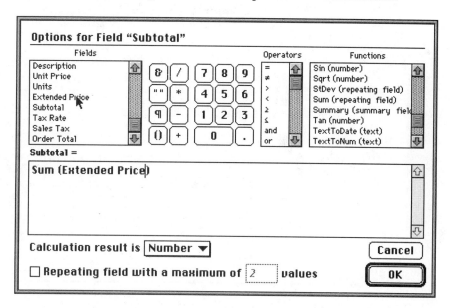

Click on OK to accept the formula. In the Define Fields dialog box, the formula appears in the Options column for that field. Click on Done to dismiss the Define Fields dialog box.

In Browse mode, the field you changed now contains the result of the formula you wrote.

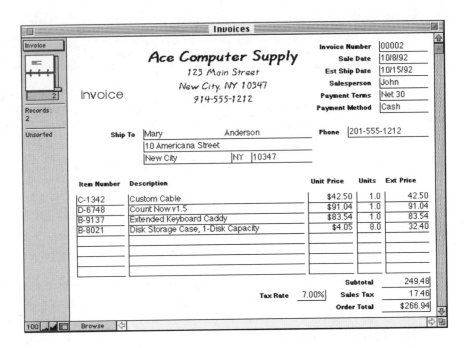

If other calculation fields use that field, their results also change. Experiment with the field by entering different values in the repeating field. You'll see the field's value change when you accept your entry by moving to another field.

USING PREDEFINED VALUE LISTS

You can use predefined lists to make sure that only acceptable values are entered into your database. However, a more powerful use of value lists is to create data-entry lists. Entering values into a field with a data-entry list is as simple as clicking or double-clicking on the option you want.

Like repeating fields, predefined value lists are created in a two-step process. The first step is to define the field to include a predefined value list. The second step is to modify the field's format to show the value list as you want it to appear.

DEFINING A VALUE LIST

A value list is best used for fields with a limited number of possible values. For example, you might want to create one that lists the names of the salespeople who use an invoices database.

Access the Define Fields dialog box and select the name of the field that you want to include a predefined value list, or create a new field. Click on Options to display the Entry Options dialog box. In that dialog box, click on the check box beside the words *Use a pre-defined value list*. Selecting this option automatically clicks the Edit Values button, and the Display Values dialog box appears.

Enter the values you want to include for the field, pressing Return after each one. The values appear in the order you enter them. If you enter more values than can fit in the edit box, the box scrolls to hold them all.

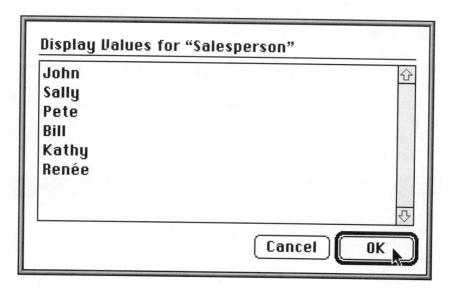

TIP

*The order you list values in the Display Values dialog box can be
used to sort that field. Sorting records is discussed in Chapter 8.*

Click on OK to accept the values and dismiss the Display Values dialog box, and
then click on OK to dismiss the Entry Options dialog box. In the Define Fields
dialog box, the words *Value List* appear in the Options column of the Field List
window for that field. Click on Done to leave the Define Fields dialog box.

The field works no differently than when it was first created. Changing the field
format in Layout mode, however, will completely change the way entries can be
made in the field.

FORMATTING A PREDEFINED VALUE LIST FIELD

You can format a field with a predefined value list to display those values in a
variety of ways: a pop-up list, a pop-up menu, check boxes, or radio buttons.
Selecting an option from displayed values makes data entry easier and helps
ensure consistency in the way data is entered.

To format a predefined value list, switch to Layout mode and click once on the
field with a value list to select it. Select Field Format from the Format menu to
access the Field Format dialog box.

In the Display Type area of the Field Format dialog box, click on the radio button
beside the words *Using a field's value list*. The option's pop-up menu becomes
active. From the pop-up menu, select the way you want the value list to appear.

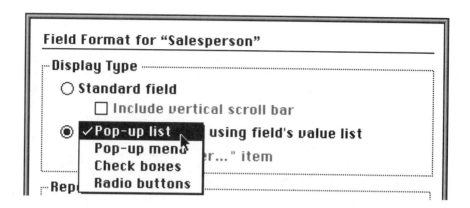

NEW IN 2.0

FileMaker Pro now allows you to add an Other option to your predefined value lists.

If you select a pop-up menu, check boxes, or radio buttons, you can also click on the check box beneath the menu to include an option called Other. This lets the user enter a value that is not included in the predefined value list. In Browse mode, selecting Other from the value list displays a dialog box for entering data.

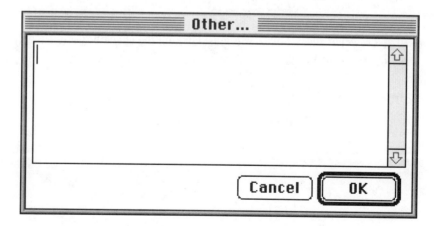

After you choose a format for your list, click on OK in the Field Format dialog box.

In Browse mode, you can select a value for the field as follows:

▸ If you selected a pop-up list, when you press the Tab key to go to the field, a list of the predefined values appears. Double-click on an option to select it and insert it in the field.

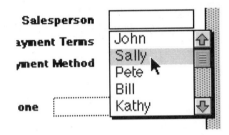

▸ If you selected a pop-up menu, you must use your mouse to pull down a menu. Select a predefined value from the menu.

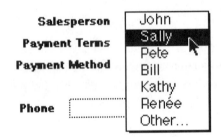

▸ If you selected check boxes, you must click on the check box immediately before the value to select it. You can select multiple check boxes.

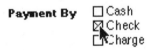

▸ If you selected radio buttons, you must click on the radio button immediately before the value to select it.

Payment By
- ⦿ Cash
- ○ Check
- ○ Charge

PERFORMING LOOKUPS

You can use FileMaker Pro's lookup feature to fill a field with information from another database file. FileMaker Pro looks up information by matching the contents of another field with the contents of a field in the lookup file. This not only saves data-entry time, but it helps ensure accuracy and consistency in fields.

WORKING WITH LOOKUP FILES AND FIELDS

Lookups involve two files and four fields. The two files are the current file and the lookup file. The *current file* is the one you are working with—the one that contains the field for which you're creating a lookup. It must be open to create the lookup.

The *lookup file* is the one you tell FileMaker Pro to look in for information. It does not need to be open. When you create the lookup, you tell FileMaker Pro what this file is called and where it is. The file can be on another computer in your network or on a floppy disk. In any case, FileMaker Pro must be able to open the file when you create the lookup and then when it is looking up information.

Lookups use four fields, two in the current file and two in the lookup file:

▸ **Destination field:** The destination field is the field in the current file that you are defining as a lookup field. It will receive the information from the lookup file.

- **Trigger field:** The trigger field is the field in the current file into which you enter a value that causes FileMaker Pro to begin the lookup procedure.

- **Source field:** The source field is the field in the lookup file that supplies the information. Its contents and field type should correspond with the contents and field type of the destination field.

- **Match field:** The match field is the field in the lookup file that FileMaker Pro will try to match with the trigger field value. Its contents and field type must correspond with the contents and field type of the trigger field.

For example, in an invoices database (the current file), you can set up the Description field (the destination field) to automatically get the description information (the source field) from a parts inventory file (the lookup file), when you enter a value in the Item Number field (the trigger field). This may seem confusing at first, but the benefits of lookups are worth the effort of figuring out how they work.

DEFINING A LOOKUP

To define a lookup field, select or create the field through the Define Fields dialog box, click on Options, and then click on the check box beside the words *Look up values from a file* (at the bottom of the Entry Options dialog box). Selecting this option automatically clicks the Set Lookup button. A standard Open File dialog box appears.

FOR MORE INFORMATION...
If you're not sure how to use the Open File dialog box, consult the reference manuals that came with your Macintosh.

Use the Open File dialog box to select and open the lookup file—the database that contains the information you want to retrieve. FileMaker Pro opens the file and reads all the field names into memory. It then displays the Lookup Value dialog box.

```
┌─────────────────────────────────────────────────────────────┐
│  Lookup Value for Field "Description"                         │
│                                                               │
│  Lookup File                    Current File                  │
│  "Parts Inventory"              "Invoices"                    │
│                                                               │
│  Copy the contents of:          ...into the field:           │
│  ┌──────────────────────┐          "Description"             │
│  │ Part Name         ▼  │                                     │
│  └──────────────────────┘                                     │
│                                                               │
│  ...when the value in:          ...matches a new entry in:    │
│  ┌──────────────────────┐       ┌──────────────────────┐     │
│  │ Part Name         ▼  │       │ Invoice Number    ▼  │     │
│  └──────────────────────┘       └──────────────────────┘     │
│                                                               │
│  ┌ If no exact match, then ┐     ☐ Don't copy contents if empty │
│  │ ◉ don't copy            │                                  │
│  │ ○ copy next lower value │                                  │
│  │ ○ copy next higher value│     ┌──────────────────────┐     │
│  │ ○ use [            ]    │     │   Set Lookup File... │     │
│  └────────────────────────┘     └──────────────────────┘     │
│                                  ( Cancel )  (   OK   )       │
└─────────────────────────────────────────────────────────────┘
```

In this dialog box, you specify the source, match, and target fields for the lookup, as follows:

▸ From the pop-up menu under *Copy the contents of*, select the source field—the field in the lookup file that contains the information you want to copy. For example, if you're copying information into the Description field of an invoices database, the source field might be the Description field in your parts inventory database.

▸ From the pop-up menu under *...when the value in*, select the match field—the field in the lookup file that contains the information you want to match in the current file. For example, if you're basing the lookup on the Item Number field in an invoices database, the match field might be the Part Number field in the parts inventory database. The fields don't need to have the same name as long as they contain the same information.

INCREASING PRODUCTIVITY
WITH FIELD-ENTRY OPTIONS
. . . .

CH. 11

◆ From the pop-up menu under ...*matches a new entry in*, select the trigger field—the field in the current file that stores the information you will enter to trigger the match. For example, to look up information based on the item number entered, choose the Item Number field as the field to match a new entry.

Review your selections in the dialog box to make sure they make sense. When you're finished with the pop-up menus, you should be able to read the options as a sentence that explains the logic of your selections. In this example, the sentence reads "Copy the contents of Description into the field Description when the value in Part Number matches the new entry in Item Number":

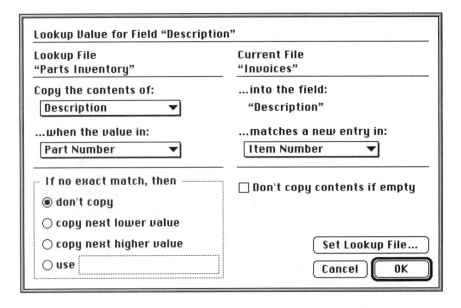

The field names appear under the name of the file that contains them.

You can use the options at the bottom of the Lookup Value dialog box to instruct FileMaker Pro what to do if it doesn't find a match. FileMaker Pro can take the following actions when it cannot match the contents of the trigger field to the match field:

▸ **Don't Copy:** Leave the destination field blank.

▸ **Copy Next Lower Value:** Use the value in the source field that corresponds to the next lower value of the match field.

▸ **Copy Next Higher Value:** Use the value in the source field that corresponds to the next higher value of the match field.

▸ **Use:** Display a message of up to 254 characters.

For example, suppose that you're looking up a discount rate in a database that contains a table of discounts. The discount rate varies depending on a Total field, but the database does not contain rates for every possible total. Choose the Copy Next Lower Value option to have FileMaker Pro find the next lowest Total field in the lookup file and use the value in the corresponding source field.

Or you may want a message to appear when FileMaker Pro can't find a match. For example, to display the message *Invalid Item Number*, click on the Use radio button and enter that text.

```
┌─ If no exact match, then ─────────────┐
│                                        │
│  ○ don't copy                          │
│                                        │
│  ○ copy next lower value               │
│                                        │
│  ○ copy next higher value              │
│                                        │
│  ◉ use │Invalid Item Number│           │
│                                        │
└────────────────────────────────────────┘
```

When you're finished, click on OK in the Lookup Value dialog box, then in the Entry Options dialog box. In the Define Fields dialog box, *Lookup* appears in the Options column of the Field List window for that field. Click on Done to dismiss the Define Fields dialog box.

WARNING

If you change values in the trigger field, FileMaker Pro does not automatically change the value in the destination field. To update that field, you must use the Relookup command on the Edit menu.

You can test the lookup by entering a value in the trigger field of the current file. For example, enter a value in the Item Number field, press Tab, and see if the correct item description appears in the Description field.

THIS CHAPTER COVERED a lot of territory. You learned about auto-entry fields, entry verification, repeating fields, predefined value lists, and lookup fields. By using field-entry options, you can ensure that the correct values are entered into the appropriate fields. You can also format value lists as pop-up lists, pop-up menus, check boxes, or radio buttons, to make data entry as easy as a click of the mouse. Your lookup fields can get information from other database files.

In the next (and last) chapter, we'll cover a few miscellaneous features of File-Maker Pro, including its new Preferences feature, importing and exporting capabilities, and some security options. We'll also take a quick look at FileMaker Pro's new ScriptMaker.

Using Advanced Features

FILEMAKER PRO INCLUDES some advanced features that you can use to make your work with the program more efficient and pleasant. In this last chapter, you'll learn how to set FileMaker Pro's Preferences options, import and export information, limit access to your files, and work with the ScriptMaker.

Although it is not especially difficult to use any of the features discussed in this chapter, a solid knowledge of Macintosh and FileMaker Pro basics will make your work easier. Refer to earlier chapters if you need to review how to accomplish routine database tasks.

SETTING PREFERENCES

You can change some of FileMaker Pro's default settings to suit your own work habits. To set preferences, select Preferences from the File menu. The Preferences dialog box appears.

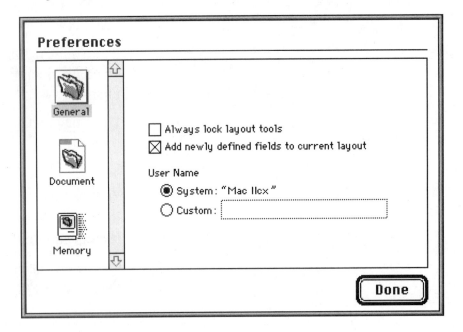

NEW IN 2.0

You can now use the Preferences dialog box to change FileMaker Pro's default settings.

On the left side of this dialog box is a narrow window with icons for the three categories of preferences: General, Document, and Memory. The wider window on the right side of the dialog box contains the settings for the currently selected category. You select the category in the left window and change the preferences in the right window. When you're finished, click on Done to accept your changes.

SETTING GENERAL PREFERENCES

When you first access the Preferences dialog box, you see the settings for the General category:

▸ **Always Lock Layout Tools:** This setting pertains to the tool palette in Layout mode. As you learned in Chapter 4, clicking on a layout tool (other than the pointer tool) selects that tool for one use only. Double-clicking on the tool locks the tool. Turning on this setting tells FileMaker Pro to always lock a layout tool for multiple use.

▸ **Add Newly Defined Fields to Current Layout:** With this setting turned on, FileMaker Pro automatically adds fields to the current layout as you define them. To prevent this from happening, turn this option off.

▸ **User Name:** This setting pertains to fields you have set to automatically include the creator or modifier name (Chapter 11 explains how to set up auto-entry fields). You have a choice of two options: the name of your computer (which should appear next to the System radio button) or the name you type in the edit box next to the Custom radio button.

SETTING DOCUMENT PREFERENCES

The Document preferences apply to the currently open document. Click on the Document icon in the Preferences dialog box, and the Document preferences

USING
ADVANCED FEATURES
. . . .

CH. 12

settings appear in the window on the right.

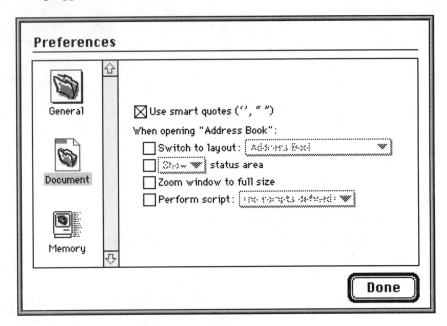

FileMaker Pro offers five options you can change:

▶ **Use Smart Quotes:** When this option is turned on, FileMaker Pro automatically substitutes smart quotes when you type regular quotation mark characters in this document. *Smart quotes* are special quotation marks that curve in toward the text they enclose. They are strictly for appearances—smart quotes simply look nicer than regular ones.

▶ **Switch to Layout:** This option lets you specify a layout to display when opening this document. When you click on this check box, the pop-up menu beside it becomes active. It lists all your existing layouts. Select the layout you want to appear when the file is opened.

▶ **Show/Hide Status Area:** This option tells FileMaker Pro to either show or hide the status area when opening the file. When you click this check box on, the pop-up menu beside it becomes active. Select from the menu's two choices: Show or Hide.

◆ **Zoom Window to Full Size:** As you work with your database, you can use the size box to change the size of the document window. FileMaker Pro remembers this size when you close the file and automatically uses the same size next time you open it. To have FileMaker Pro always open the file with a full-size window, click this check box on.

FOR MORE INFORMATION...
If you're not familiar with the standard Macintosh size box, consult the manuals that came with your Macintosh.

◆ **Perform Script:** If your database file includes scripts, you can use this option to have FileMaker Pro perform one of them when you open the file. Scripts automate tasks. You create them with FileMaker Pro's ScriptMaker, as explained later in the chapter. When you click this check box on, the pop-up menu beside it becomes active. This menu includes all the scripts defined for the database.

SETTING MEMORY PREFERENCES

As you work with FileMaker Pro, the changes you make are saved to the computer's random access memory (RAM) in a special area called a *cache*. FileMaker Pro automatically saves the contents of the cache to disk. The Memory preferences let you tell FileMaker Pro how often to save your changes. This is especially useful for PowerBook users who need to conserve battery power. Each time FileMaker Pro saves changes, it uses power, running down the battery little by little.

To access the Memory preferences, click on the Memory icon in the Preferences dialog box. The right window changes to display the Memory preferences.

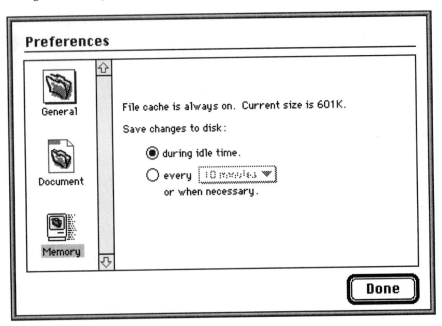

You can set FileMaker Pro to save changes to disk either during idle time or at the interval you specify. No matter which option you select, FileMaker Pro will save changes to disk any time the cache fills.

The During Idle Time radio button instructs FileMaker Pro to save changes when you aren't working. This is the default setting.

When you choose the Every radio button, the pop-up menu beside it becomes active. It lists your choices for the time interval for saving the file.

TIP

PowerBook users may want to select the highest interval for saving changes to disk. Saving less often conserves battery power.

IMPORTING AND EXPORTING INFORMATION

Sometimes the information you want to include in your database already exists in another file. Other times, you may want to include the information in your File-Maker Pro file in another file. Rather than reenter all the records manually, you can use FileMaker Pro's commands for importing (bringing in information) and exporting (transferring information to another file) files. Using these commands can save you time and effort when you're exchanging records between documents, especially when dealing with many records.

FileMaker Pro recognizes a number of file formats (other than the FileMaker Pro format, of course) for importing and exporting records. The most common format for database and spreadsheet files is tab-separated text. In this text file format, each field is separated from the next by a tab character, and each record is separated from the next by a return character. The file must contain the same number of fields for each record, and each record's fields must be in the same order. Most database and spreadsheet applications can export files in this format.

Here's an example of a Microsoft Word text file ready to be imported into File-Maker Pro:

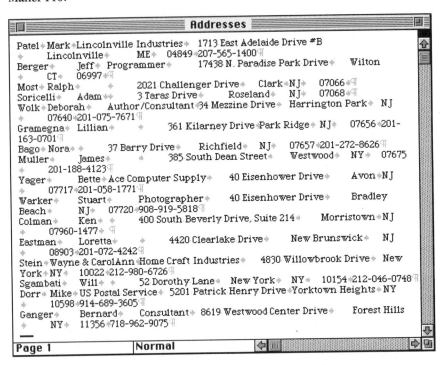

In this example, the gray arrows are tab characters and the backwards *P*s are return characters. Notice that where field information is missing, a tab character still marks the end of the field.

FileMaker Pro also recognizes these file formats:

▸ **Comma-separated text:** This text format file is just like the tab-separated text format, but commas separate the fields rather than tabs. If a field includes a comma, the field should be enclosed in quotation marks.

▸ **SYLK:** SYLK stands for Symbolic Link Format. This kind of file stores information in columns and rows. It is a popular format for spreadsheet applications.

▸ **DBF:** This is a format to use with dBASE III files. dBASE III is a popular MS DOS database application.

- **DIF:** DIF stands for Data Interchange Format. Like SYLK, it stores information in columns and rows. It is used by some spreadsheet applications, such as VisiCalc and the AppleWorks spreadsheet module.

- **WKS:** This is a Lotus 1-2-3 file format. Lotus 1-2-3 is a popular spreadsheet application for both Macintosh and MS DOS platforms.

- **BASIC:** This text format file is similar to the comma-separated text format, but it conforms to the Microsoft BASIC standards. This format is generated by many BASIC programs.

- **Merge:** This text file format is similar to the tab-separated text format, but it includes a *header record* of field names that can be used by the mail merge features of many word processing applications. For this reason, it's a good format to use when exporting records for a mail merge.

- **Data Access Manager:** This is a highly specialized query document created with a third-party query program. It is used for importing data from another database.

- **Edition File:** This is an export-only format similar to tab-separated text. Edition files can be subscribed to by System 7 users using applications that support the Edition Manager.

NOTE

Data queries and edition files are special features for advanced FileMaker Pro users.

The formats you'll probably work with most often are tab-separated text, comma-separated text, and merge.

IMPORTING RECORDS

The Import Records command on the File menu lets you add records stored in another file, called the *source file*, to a FileMaker Pro database, called the *destination file*. The source file must be in one of the formats listed above.

Create or open a FileMaker Pro file to import the information into. The database file should have fields corresponding to the fields in the text file. The fields do not need to be in the same order.

To import data, select Import/Export from the File menu, and then choose Import Records from the submenu that pops out.

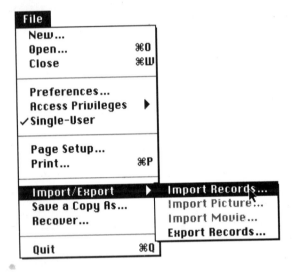

A standard Open File Dialog box appears. It includes a File Type pop-up menu. Use this menu to select the type of file you are importing.

Locate the file in the file list scrolling window and click on Open. The Specify Field Order for Import dialog box appears.

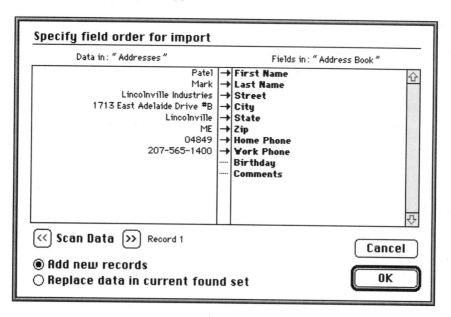

This dialog box has a main scrolling window split into two parts. The left side displays the first record of the file you are importing. The right side displays the field names in your FileMaker Pro file. As in the example above, the order of the fields in the source file may not match the order of the fields in the destination file. In addition, either file may include fields that the other does not include.

Between the two halves of the main window is a column of arrows and dotted lines. The arrows tell you what field on the left will be imported into each field on the right. The dotted lines are beside fields that will not be imported.

Change the order of the fields on the right by dragging them up or down in the field order. Click on the arrows between the two halves of the main window to turn them on (arrows) or off (dotted lines). Any field on the left that you do not want imported should have dotted lines rather than an arrow beside it. You can use the Scan Data arrows to scroll through each record of the source file on the left. This may help you match data to fields in the destination file. When you're finished, the fields on the left should match up with the field names on the right, as in this example:

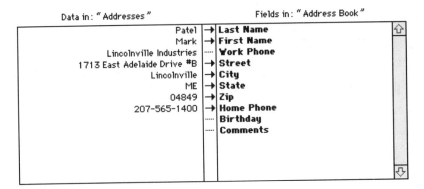

After you specify the field order, click on the appropriate radio button for the way you want the data imported:

- **Add New Records:** This option adds the records to those already existing in the database. Those new records then become the found set (the records located by a find request, as described in Chapter 7).

WARNING
When you replace data in the current found set, your action cannot be undone. Use this option with caution!

- **Replace Data in Current Found Set:** This option deletes the records in the found set and then adds the records in the source file.

Click on OK to import the records. A message box appears, showing FileMaker Pro's progress.

```
Importing from:
"Addresses".

[████████████████████████            ]

Total records imported:  10
To cancel, hold down the ⌘ key and type
a period (.).
```

When this message box disappears, the records are imported and displayed as the found set.

EXPORTING RECORDS

The Export Records command on the File menu lets you create a new file containing FileMaker Pro database records. This file, which is called the destination file, must be in one of the formats listed earlier in the chapter.

Open the FileMaker Pro file containing the records you want to export. If you want to export only some of the records, use the Find command to select those records (see Chapter 7). If you want the records to be exported in a certain order, use the Sort command to sort them (see Chapter 8).

From the File menu, select Import/Export. Select Export Records from the submenu that pops out. A standard Save As dialog box appears. It includes a File Type pop-up menu you can use to select the type of file you want to create, which lists the same formats as the File Type pop-up menu you see when importing records. Select the correct file type, then enter a file name in the Export To edit box and click on New. The Specify Field Order for Export dialog box appears.

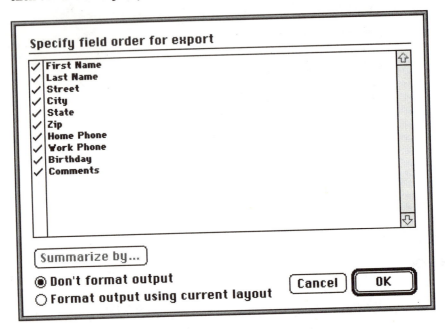

This dialog box displays the field names in your FileMaker Pro file. Check marks to the left of each field name indicate that the field will be exported.

Change the order of the fields by dragging them up or down in the field order. Click on the check marks to turn them on or off. When you're finished, the fields you want to include should be in the order you want in the new file.

Specify field order for export

✓ Last Name
✓ First Name
✓ Street
✓ City
✓ State
✓ Zip
✓ Home Phone
✓ Work Phone
✓ Birthday
✓ Comments

If your database includes summary fields and has been properly sorted to summarize data by these fields, you can export summary information (see Chapter 10 for information about summary fields). Click on a summary field to select it and then click on the Summarize By button. The Summarize By dialog box appears.

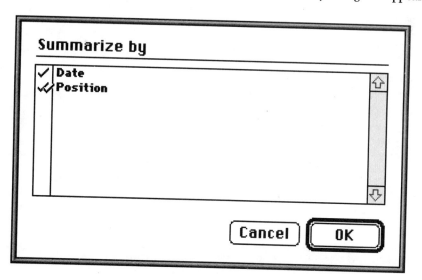

Summarize by

✓ Date
✓ Position

Cancel   OK

NEW IN 2.0

FileMaker Pro can now export summary information.

Check the fields you want to summarize by, then click on OK. Your selections appear in the Specify Field Order for Export dialog box.

Specify field order for export

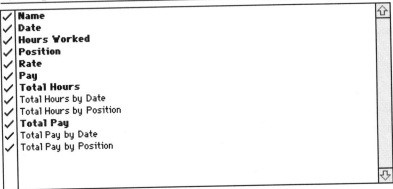

Click on the appropriate radio button to tell FileMaker Pro whether or not it should format the output:

▸ **Don't Format Output:** When this option is selected, FileMaker Pro will export numbers, dates, and times just the way they were entered into the database.

▸ **Format Output Using Current Layout:** When this option is selected, FileMaker Pro will export numbers, dates, and times the way they are formatted in the current layout.

Click on OK to export the records. A message box appears, showing you FileMaker Pro's progress.

```
Exporting to:
"NJ Addresses".

[▓▓▓▓▓▓▓▓▓▓▓▓▓                        ]

Records remaining to export:  45
To cancel, hold down the ⌘ key and type
a period (.).
```

When this message box disappears, you'll have a new file on your disk with the information that was exported from your database.

CONTROLLING ACCESS TO FILES

To limit access to database files, you can define access privileges in FileMaker Pro. This feature lets you determine what a user can do with a file based on passwords and groups. You can base user access on activities, such as browsing and editing records and creating or modifying layouts, as well as on layouts and fields.

Although you can define access privileges in a wide variety of ways, we'll concentrate on three common access-limitation requirements: password-protecting a file, allowing read-only access to a file, and allowing access to only some fields and layouts. You can use the techniques covered here to create your own access controls.

PASSWORD-PROTECTING A FILE

The contents of some database files may be confidential. When you password-protect your files, they cannot be opened by users without the proper password.

Password protection begins wtih a master password that allows all access privileges for a file. From the File menu, select Access Privileges, and then choose Define Passwords from the submenu that appears.

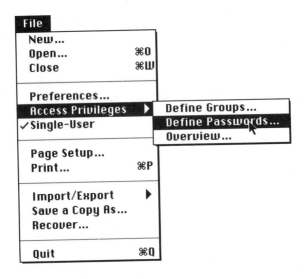

The Define Passwords dialog box appears.

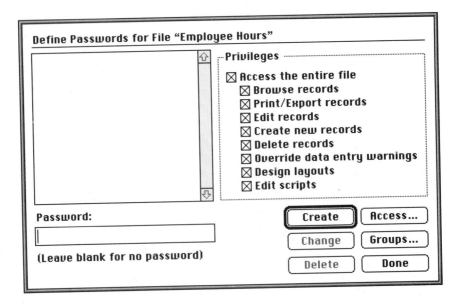

This dialog box lets you specify passwords and related activities.

In the Password edit box, enter the password you want to use to protect your file. This will be the master password. Make sure *all* the check boxes on the Privileges side of the dialog box are checked. These check boxes indicate what a user with the master password can do. Then click on Create. The password appears in the left window of the dialog box. Click on Done. A dialog box appears, asking you to confirm that you know a password to access the entire file.

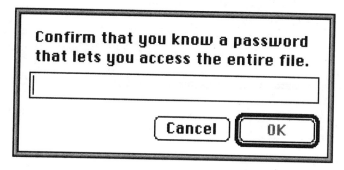

Type in the password (a bullet appears for each character) and click on OK. You are returned to your database file.

WARNING

Once you close your database file, the password is required to reopen it. If you forget the password, the file cannot be reopened! Write down the password so you don't forget it.

To make sure the password works, close the file, then use the Open command from the File menu to open it. FileMaker Pro prompts you for a password with a dialog box like this:

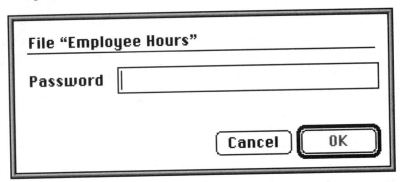

File "Employee Hours"

Password

Cancel   OK

Type in the password (once again, a bullet appears for each character) and click on OK. If you enter an incorrect password, FileMaker Pro lets you know.

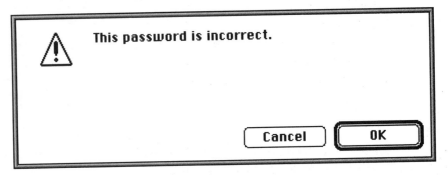

⚠ This password is incorrect.

Cancel   OK

You will not be able to access the file until you enter the correct password.

ALLOWING READ-ONLY ACCESS TO A FILE

You may have a database file that you need to share, but you don't want others to edit that file. You can create another password that lets the user open the file, browse through its contents, and print the file—but not make a single change to it.

To create a read-only password, select Access Privileges from the File menu, and choose Define Passwords from the submenu. In the Password edit box of the Define Passwords dialog box, enter the password you want to give users so that they can browse and print the file. If you prefer, you can leave the Password edit box blank so that no password is required for limited access.

On the Privileges side of the dialog box, make sure the only two check boxes with checks are the ones for Browse Records and Print/Export Records. Click on Create, and the password appears in the left window of the dialog box.

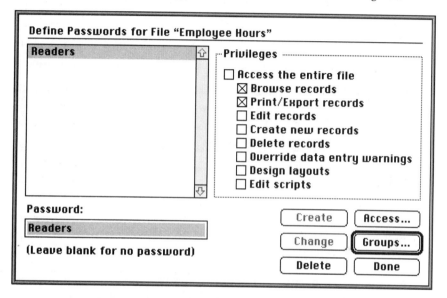

Click on Done. If you already created a master password for this file, a read-only password is established.

If you did not create a master password, FileMaker Pro warns you that no one has access to the whole file.

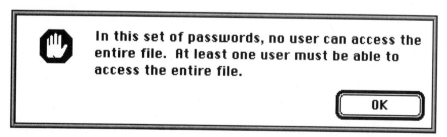

Click on OK in the warning dialog box and set up a master password for the file, as described in the previous section. When you click on Done after creating the master password, a dialog box appears, asking you to confirm that you know a password to access the entire file. Type in the master password and click on OK. You are returned to your database file.

To make sure the read-only protection works, close the file, then use the Open command from the File menu to reopen it. If you left the Password edit box blank so that a password is not required, the password prompt will appear like this:

If a password is required, FileMaker Pro prompts you for it. Type in the limited access password (a bullet appears for each character) and click on OK. If you enter an incorrect password, you won't be able to open the file.

After you access the file with a limited access password, try working with that database. You'll see that your activities are greatly limited.

LIMITING ACCESS TO DATABASE FIELDS AND LAYOUTS

NOTE
To make changes to access privileges, you must use the master password when opening the file.

To limit access to actual fields and layouts, you must specify access privileges for a group and associate the group with a password. Select Access Privileges from the File menu, and then choose Define Groups from the submenu. The Define Groups dialog box appears.

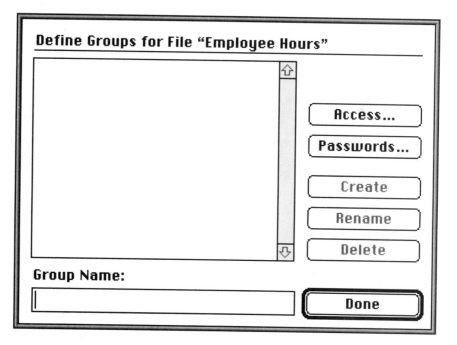

Enter the name of a group you want to define and click on Create. The group name appears in the Group List window. Click on Access. The Access Privileges Dialog box appears.

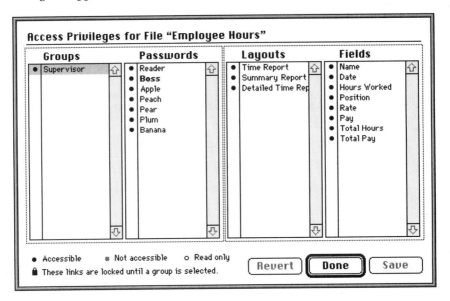

This dialog box lists groups, passwords, layouts, and fields.

With the group you just defined selected, use your mouse pointer to associate passwords with the group. Click on the bullet in front of the passwords. The mouse pointer turns into a check mark and toggles the bullet from black to gray.

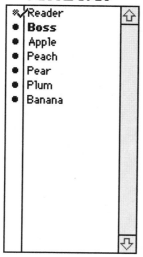

A black bullet means the password is associated with the selected group. A gray bullet means the password is not associated with the group.

Next use the same technique to assign layout and field privileges to the selected group. When you click on the bullet beside a layout or field name, the mouse pointer again turns into a check mark.

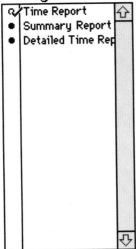

Click to change the bullet to one of the three possible access privileges:

▸ A black bullet means the layout or field is accessible.

▸ A hollow bullet means the layout or field is read-only (it cannot be modified).

▸ A gray bullet means the layout or field is not accessible at all.

Your assignments may look something like this:

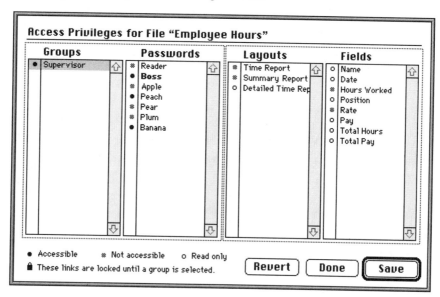

In this example, the people with the passwords Peach and Banana are supervisors who have read-only access to one layout and four fields. Through the Define Passwords dialog box, their passwords were defined with browse and print privileges only.

After you're finished, click on Save to save the settings, then click on Done to dismiss the Access Privileges dialog box. Finally, click on Done in the Define Groups dialog box.

Test the group to make sure it works. Close the file, and then reopen it. When File-Maker Pro prompts you, type in a password associated with the group you just created. Notice the differences in the way FileMaker Pro looks.

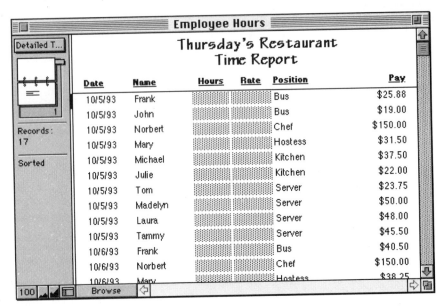

Fields that are not accessible are gray. If you try to access a layout that is not accessible to the group, the words *Access Denied* appear in the document window. The Define Fields command under the Select menu is gray. The file is locked tight, just the way you set it up.

INTRODUCING SCRIPTMAKER

NEW IN 2.0

ScriptMaker is a new feature. Previous versions of FileMaker Pro had very limited scripting capabilities.

The ScriptMaker is FileMaker Pro's new script-writing utility. With it, you can instruct FileMaker Pro to perform a series of actions when you issue just one command. Scripts automate repeated tasks and simplify your work. Since FileMaker Pro can include your scripts (up to 52 of them) on its Scripts menu, they're easy to access.

The ScriptMaker writes scripts for you based on the actions you took before selecting the ScriptMaker command on the Scripts menu. You can accept the script as is, edit it to work differently, or clear it and write your own.

To give you an idea of what you can do with the ScriptMaker, the following sections describe how to create scripts for two common database chores: printing mailing labels and setting up reports.

CREATING A MAILING LABELS SCRIPT

If you use FileMaker Pro to manage your mailing lists, a mailing labels script can make your work more efficient. This type of script will automatically generate mailing labels sorted by zip code.

NOTE
*To create a mailing labels script, you need a mailing label layout.
If one does not exist, create one, as described in Chapter 6.*

Use the Layout pop-up menu to switch to a mailing label layout. Then use the Sort command to sort by zip code (see Chapter 8).

From the Scripts menu, select ScriptMaker. The Define Scripts dialog box appears.

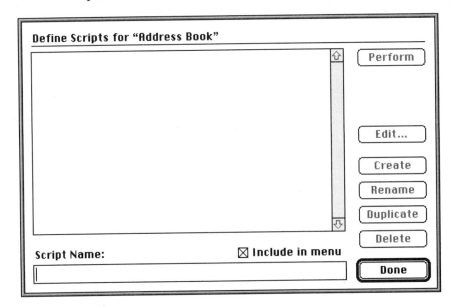

Enter a name for your script in the Script Name edit box. If you want the script to appear on the Scripts menu, make sure the Include in Menu check box is clicked on. Click on Create. The script name appears in the Scripts List window, and the

Script Definition dialog box appears.

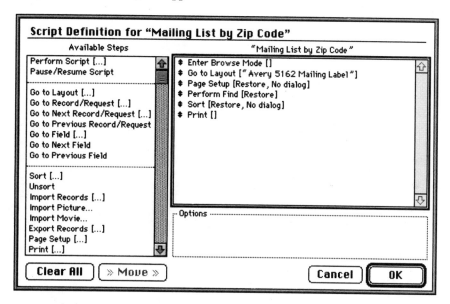

```
Script Definition for "Mailing List by Zip Code"
    Available Steps                    "Mailing List by Zip Code"
  Perform Script [...]              ↕ Enter Browse Mode []
  Pause/Resume Script               ↕ Go to Layout ["Avery 5162 Mailing Label"]
  ............................      ↕ Page Setup [Restore, No dialog]
  Go to Layout [...]                ↕ Perform Find [Restore]
  Go to Record/Request [...]        ↕ Sort [Restore, No dialog]
  Go to Next Record/Request [...]   ↕ Print []
  Go to Previous Record/Request
  Go to Field [...]
  Go to Next Field
  Go to Previous Field
  ............................
  Sort [...]
  Unsort
  Import Records [...]              ┌ Options ─────────────────────
  Import Picture...
  Import Movie...
  Export Records [...]
  Page Setup [...]
  Print [...]
  [ Clear All ]  [ » Move » ]           [ Cancel ]  [ OK ]
```

This dialog box has three main parts:

▸ **Available Steps:** This window, on the left side of the dialog box, lists all the steps you can include in a script.

▸ **Current Script**: This window, on the right side of the dialog box, shows the current script, which has been preset by FileMaker Pro.

▸ **Options:** Below the current script is an Options window. Depending on the script step selected, options for that step may appear here.

The preset script shown in the example above includes all the steps you need to perform to create your mailing lists. Each line contains a command, which may include options between brackets ([]). Clicking on a command displays the available options for that command.

Let's take a look at the commands in the mailing list script FileMaker Pro wrote. The first command

Enter Browse Mode []

instructs FileMaker Pro to switch to Browse mode. There is only one possible option, and it has not been checked:

```
┌─ Options ──────────────────────────────────────────────┐
│                                                         │
│   ☐ Pause                                               │
│                                                         │
└─────────────────────────────────────────────────────────┘
```

If you checked the Pause option, the script would stop after switching to Browse mode and wait for the user to click on Continue. Then the script would continue with the next command.

The second command

> Go to Layout ["Avery 5162 Mailing Label"]

instructs FileMaker Pro to switch to the label layout. This command has two options:

```
┌─ Options ──────────────────────────────────────────────┐
│   ☐ Refresh screen                                      │
│                                                         │
│              Specify : ┌─ Avery 5162 Maili...▼ ┐        │
└─────────────────────────────────────────────────────────┘
```

The Refresh Screen command ensures that the layout is displayed properly in the document window. The Specify menu lists your layouts.

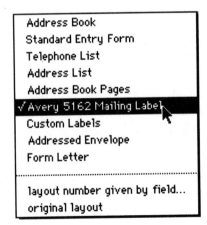

On the third line, the command

> Page Setup [Restore, No dialog]

instructs FileMaker Pro to restore settings in the Page Setup dialog box to the way they were when the script was created. This command has two options:

> ┌ Options ───
> │ ☒ Restore setup options
> │ ☒ Perform without dialog
> └──

If you turned off these options, the script's original Page Setup settings would not be restored, and the Page Setup dialog box would appear.

The next command

> Perform Find [Restore]

tells FileMaker Pro to perform the Find command using the find request last used when the script was created. Its single option is checked:

> ┌ Options ───
> │ ☒ Restore find requests
> │
> └──

The command for sorting the mailing list is

> Sort [Restore, No dialog]

which instructs FileMaker Pro to sort the records using the sort order in memory when the script was created. In this example, the database was last sorted by the

Zip Code field, so that's the sort order FileMaker Pro will use with this script. Both of this command's options are checked:

```
┌─ Options ──────────────────────────────────────────────────────┐
:                                                                  :
:    ⊠ Restore sort order                                         :
:    ⊠ Perform without dialog                                     :
:                                                                  :
└──────────────────────────────────────────────────────────────────┘
```

The final command in the script is

    Print[]

which tells FileMaker Pro to print the records. It has one option:

```
┌─ Options ──────────────────────────────────────────────────────┐
:                                                                  :
:                                                                  :
:    ☐ Perform without dialog                                     :
:                                                                  :
└──────────────────────────────────────────────────────────────────┘
```

Because this option isn't checked, the Print dialog box appears. You can specify print options and make sure your printer is ready.

If you click on OK in the Script Definition dialog box, FileMaker Pro saves the script as it is. However, the mailing labels script needs one change.

EDITING THE PRESET SCRIPT

In this example, the mailing labels script should always print all the records in the database, so you need to replace the Perform Find command with the Find All command.

To clear the Perform Find command, click on it in the Current Script scrolling window, and then click on the Clear button. In the Available Steps scrolling window, scroll down until you find the command Find All. Click once on the command to select it, and click on Move to move it to the Current Script scrolling window.

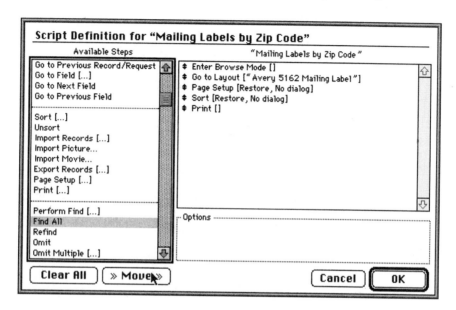

SHORTCUT

Double-clicking on a command in the Available Steps window selects it and moves it to the Current Script window in one step.

Place your mouse pointer over the double-arrow icon to the left of the Find All command, press the mouse button, and drag the command.

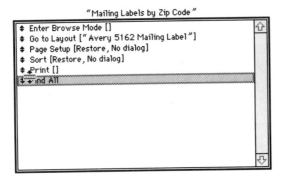

Position Find All above the Sort command and release the mouse button.

Click on OK in the Script Definition dialog box to save the script.

To test the script, pull down the Scripts menu and select the script name from the menu. If you did not add the script to the menu, choose ScriptMaker from the Scripts menu, select the script in the Script List window, and click on Perform.

WRITING A REPORT SCRIPT

You can use the ScriptMaker to write your own scripts from scratch. For example, suppose that you want to view a phone list of all the records of people who live in California. Since your phone list layout does not include the State field, you need to use another layout to make your record selection. You can create a script to change to that layout, then sort the records by the Last Name and First Name fields, change to your phone list layout, hide the status area to maximize the viewing area, and preview the results.

From the Scripts menu, select ScriptMaker. Enter a name for the script in the Script Name edit box, make sure the Include in Menu check box is clicked on, and click on Create. In the Script Definition dialog box, click on the Clear All button to erase the preset script.

Select each command for the script from the Available Steps window and move it into the Current Script window, either by clicking on the command and then on the Move button, or by double-clicking on a command in the Available Steps window. Specify the following options in the order shown:

COMMAND	OPTIONS
Enter Browse Mode [...]	None
Go to Layout [...]	Select a layout that includes the State field from the Specify pop-up menu.
Perform Find [...]	The Restore option should be checked.
Sort [...]	The Restore and No Dialog options should be checked.
Go to Layout [...]	Select the phone list layout from the Specify pop-up menu.
Toggle Status Area [...]	Select Hide from the pop-up menu.
Enter Preview Mode [...]	The Pause option should be checked.
Toggle Status Area [...]	Select Show from the pop-up menu.
Enter Browse Mode [...]	None

Check the steps in the Current Script window. They should look something like this:

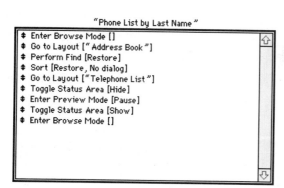

```
                "Phone List by Last Name "
⬍ Enter Browse Mode []                          ⇧
⬍ Go to Layout [" Address Book "]
⬍ Perform Find [Restore]
⬍ Sort [Restore, No dialog]
⬍ Go to Layout [" Telephone List "]
⬍ Toggle Status Area [Hide]
⬍ Enter Preview Mode [Pause]
⬍ Toggle Status Area [Show]
⬍ Enter Browse Mode []
                                                ⇩
```

**USING
ADVANCED FEATURES**

· ·

CH. 12

Click on OK to accept the script and dismiss the Script Definition dialog box. Click on Done to dismiss the Define Scripts dialog box.

Test the script by selecting it from the Scripts menu. FileMaker Pro automatically performs all the steps you specified and displays the resulting list in Preview mode. To exit Preview mode and complete the script, press the Return or Enter key.

THIS CHAPTER COVERED several of the more advanced features of FileMaker Pro. You learned how to customize some of the ways that FileMaker Pro works by changing Preferences. You explored methods for transferring information between FileMaker Pro and other applications. The chapter also described how you can use access privileges and passwords to protect your database information. Finally, you were introduced to the ScriptMaker, a powerful FileMaker Pro utility for writing scripts.

The first nine chapters of this book presented the basics of using FileMaker Pro— the information you need to use the program on a day-to-day basis. Chapters 10, 11, and 12 presented more advanced information that you'll probably want to take advantage of once you're comfortable working with FileMaker Pro. Although this book hasn't discussed every single FileMaker Pro feature, it did cover a lot of ground. As you've seen, FileMaker Pro is a user-friendly application that is easy to learn, flexible, and powerful enough for most everyday applications. Now that you've read this book, you're well on your way to becoming a FileMaker Pro expert.

INDEX

Note to the Reader:
Boldfaced page numbers indicate topics discussed in the primary subsections of each chapter. Italic page numbers indicate illustrations.

SYMBOLS

& (ampersand), 20
* (asterisk)
  in field names, 20
  as wildcard symbol, 118
@ (at sign), as wildcard symbol, 118
[] (brackets), in scripts, 245
^ (caret), 20
: (colon), for current time, 80
, (comma), 20
… (ellipsis), as range symbol, 117
= (equal)
  as exact match symbol, 117
  in field names, 20
! (exclamation point), as duplicates
    symbol, 117
> (greater than)
  in field names, 20
  in find requests, 117
>= (greater than or equal to)
  in field names, 20
  in find requests, 117
- (hyphen), 20
< (less than)
  in field names, 20
  in find requests, 116
<= (less than or equal to)
  in field names, 20

in find requests, 117
– (minus sign), for current date entry, 33
+ (plus sign), 20
# (pound sign), for page numbers, 80
? (question mark), as invalid date or time
    symbol, 118
" " (quotation marks)
  as literal text symbol, 118
  smart quotes option, 218
; (semicolon), for current time entry, 33
' (single quote),
  copying previous record with, 33
  smart quotes option, 218
// (slashes)
  in field names, 20
  as today's date symbol, 80, 118

A

access privileges. *See* passwords
Access Privileges command, 232, *232*, 234,
    237
Access Privileges dialog box, 238–241, *238*
accessing
  calculation fields, 32
  Number Format dialog box, 61

D

E

F

G

H

I

Help Yourself with
Another Quality Sybex Book

Help Yourself with Another Quality Sybex Book

Macintosh System 7 at Your Fingertips
Nancy B. Dannenberg

This quick-reference guide is a must for System 7 users. It offers fast access to concise information on every feature of the system, with reference entries organized alphabetically by topic. Perfect for experienced users seeking brief explanations of new features or for anyone who sometimes needs a quick answer on the job. Includes an overview of new features.

235pp; 4 3/4" x 8"
ISBN: 0-7821-1001-0

Available
at Better
Bookstores
Everywhere

Sybex Inc.
2021 Challenger Drive
Alameda, CA 94501
Telephone (800) 227-2346
Fax (510) 523-2373

Sybex. Help Yourself.

SYBEX

FREE BROCHURE!

Complete this form today, and we'll send you a full-color brochure of Sybex bestsellers.

Please supply the name of the Sybex book purchased.

_____

How would you rate it?

_____ Excellent   _____ Very Good   _____ Average   _____ Poor

Why did you select this particular book?

_____ Recommended to me by a friend

_____ Recommended to me by store personnel

_____ Saw an advertisement in _____

_____ Author's reputation

_____ Saw in Sybex catalog

_____ Required textbook

_____ Sybex reputation

_____ Read book review in _____

_____ In-store display

_____ Other _____

Where did you buy it?

_____ Bookstore

_____ Computer Store or Software Store

_____ Catalog (name: _____)

_____ Direct from Sybex

_____ Other: _____

Did you buy this book with your personal funds?

_____ Yes   _____ No

About how many computer books do you buy each year?

_____ 1-3   _____ 3-5   _____ 5-7   _____ 7-9   _____ 10+

About how many Sybex books do you own?

_____ 1-3   _____ 3-5   _____ 5-7   _____ 7-9   _____ 10+

Please indicate your level of experience with the software covered in this book:

_____ Beginner   _____ Intermediate   _____ Advanced

Which types of software packages do you use regularly?

_____ Accounting   _____ Databases   _____ Networks

_____ Amiga   _____ Desktop Publishing   _____ Operating Systems

_____ Apple/Mac   _____ File Utilities   _____ Spreadsheets

_____ CAD   _____ Money Management   _____ Word Processing

_____ Communications   _____ Languages   _____ Other _____

                                                                    (please specify)

Which of the following best describes your job title?

_____ Administrative/Secretarial   _____ President/CEO

_____ Director   _____ Manager/Supervisor

_____ Engineer/Technician   _____ Other _____

(please specify)

Comments on the weaknesses/strengths of this book: _____

_____

_____

_____

_____

Name _____

Street _____

City/State/Zip _____

Phone _____

PLEASE FOLD, SEAL, AND MAIL TO SYBEX

SYBEX, INC.
Department M
2021 CHALLENGER DR.
ALAMEDA, CALIFORNIA USA
94501

SYBEX

SEAL

Format Menu

Style Plain	⌘–Shift-P
Style Bold	⌘–Shift-B
Style Italic	⌘–Shift-I
Style Outline	⌘–Shift-O
Style Shadow	⌘–Shift-S
Style Underline	⌘–Shift-U
Style Superscript	⌘–Shift-+ (plus sign)
Style Subscript	⌘–Shift-– (hyphen)
Align Text Left	⌘–[(left bracket)
Align Text Center	⌘–\ (back-slash)
Align Text Right	⌘–] (right bracket)
Align Text Full	⌘–Shift-\ (back-slash)
Field Borders	⌘–Option-B
Field Format	⌘–Option-F